FLY FISHING
for GOLD

This page intentionally left blank :)

Fly Fishing for Gold

Searching for the end of Forrest Fenn's Rainbow
and his Treasure

Jeff Uryjasz

This book is dedicated to Forrest Fenn

Thank you for lighting a "blaze" under my ass
which propelled me on the adventure of a lifetime.

"My church is in the mountains and along the river
bottoms where dream's and fantasies alike go to play"
Forrest Fenn

TABLE OF CONTENTS

NOT A PREFACE

1. I AM NOT A WRITER.
and
2. TECHNICALLY I AM NOW SEEING AS I WROTE THIS.

Considering this is my first book and I know I am going to make some mistakes or break some sort of rules of writing (even though they say rules are meant to be broken), I really wanted a "Preface" since it looks and sounds more "official", but my research shows that most people tend to skip right past it to get to the substance or "THE MEAT AND POTATOES" of a book. I think they are either scared of it, don't understand it, or just don't care that it's there. Ok, so then this is not a preface, but more of an Introduction.

I am almost 47 now. Yes, that means I am currently 46 years old.

almost 47 = 46 (or somewhere between 46 and 47)

If that sounds vaguely similar to how Forrest Fenn opens his first memoir "The Thrill of the Chase", that is because it is. The reason I also chose to write it that way was not to copy, plagiarize, poach, or steal Fenn's phrasing, but to call out its importance, at least to me, and my eventual solution to his poem. I will get more into detail about that later. All I have to say right now is "I hope you are hungry".

Like many other searchers, I have known about Fenn and his hidden treasure since the release of his first memoir "The Thrill of the Chase", but at that time I thought it was just some marketing ploy by a crazy old coot (just kidding Forrest) looking to sell his book and that no one in their right mind would really hide something that valuable, especially during an economic recession. Then, after a little digging, I found out that Fenn wasn't making one cent off the book and that he even ate all the publishing costs. On top of that, the profit was being divided up between a charity, the publisher, and the only bookstore (The Collected Works Bookstore in New Mexico) that sells his book. Although, now you can also find it on Amazon or eBay if you're willing to shell out the cash. After hearing that, it elevated my interest in Fenn and his treasure a little more, so I decided to purchase his book "The Thrill of the Chase". I figured that reading the book wouldn't change anything. It's not like I was going to ever plan a trip to the Rocky Mountains to search for a patinaed bronze treasure chest the size of a shoe box…now that would be crazy. I mean, I have never been much of an adventurer or outdoorsman having spent most of my career behind a desk with my face glued to a computer screen. It was just something I had to do being that my education and employment background included; Architecture, Civil Engineering, and Land Surveying. So, you are probably wondering how Fenn baited me into adding "Treasure Hunter" to my resume.

NOT A PREFACE

I once heard Fenn say he felt like an Architect constructing the poem and that the poem with its nine clues is really a map which if solved correctly and followed precisely would give you directions to the end of his rainbow and the treasure. I thought, maybe all that education and experience I have would come in handy on something like this, so I proceeded to read his book and began analyzing it and the poem within it. But, reading a book is the easy part. It's mustering up the confidence and courage to physically go out into the mountains to search for a hidden treasure. So, why did I go?

Well, the first and most obvious reason is, who wouldn't want to go on a treasure hunt with the possibility of finding a real treasure chest full of gold and more? That should be an eye-opening proposition for anyone, except for my brother-in law Jim, and maybe my two nieces who always seem to be busy multi-tasking as they sit comfortably sunken into their couch cushions texting on their phone and watching a video on their tablet at the same time. I guess not everyone is willing to get up off the couch, get outside, and go hiking through the Rocky Mountains looking for hidden treasure.

I, on the other hand, have always enjoyed reading books like "Huckleberry Finn" and "Treasure Island" or watching treasure hunting movies like "Indian Jones", "National Treasure", and even "The Goonies". They stirred my emotions and sparked my imagination. So, given the opportunity to experience a similar adventure is something I personally could not pass up.

I do have to admit a second reason for going is that there have been many times I found myself not being able to be pried away from some of those electronic gadgets and gizmos...go figure. You see, I have the same belief as Fenn regarding the damaging affects technology and all those electronic devices are having on the younger generations. Almost everyone, now-a-days, see the world through their electronic devices and even communicate to each other through those same devices. At the beginning, I thought the growth of this type of technology was supposed to be a good thing, but are we really progressing forward?

Think about it this way. In early times, cave men used grunting and cave drawings as a form of communication. From there came petroglyphs and hieroglyphics. Many years later, as civilization progressed, people began to actually speak to each other face-to-face, and boy do I miss those days. With the invention of the telephone straight through to the time of mobile phones we spoke to people through a plethora of electronic devices. While we couldn't see people's faces during these conversations, at least we still got to hear their voices. Then when voicemail was created, we gave up our ability to see and talk to someone directly. Instead we received a digital recorded message of their voice to play at a later time. As cell phones graduated and became smart phones we didn't even have to talk anymore. Email allowed us to send a typed message to someone so they could access it at their earliest convenience. But that took too long, so we came up with texting so that those written messages would be instantly brought to our attention. Somehow that became too much work for the person sending the message though, so we had to start abbreviation everything.

"IMHO GO ISO THE TREAS BC ATEOTD YOLO"

Don't worry, I will save you the time.

"In my humble opinion, go in search of the treasure because, at the end of the day, you only live once."

And where are we at currently? Poop emojis (insert face palm here). So, if you ever meet me and hear me grunting you know why. At this point I am starting to think "I need to get off the couch and go outside."

Ultimately, after years of arm-chairing the poem, letting every-day life get in the way, and desperately needing a vacation, I was willing to put on a brave face and put down those devices, get off the couch, get outside, and confidently go traverse the Rocky Mountains and search for Fenn's treasure.

But why write a book revealing all of my thoughts, interpretations, and solutions?

I figured writing a book would be a great way for me to document the pages and pages of information I had accumulated about Fenn and also because maybe my thoughts, interpretations, and solutions to the poem would inspire others to: conjure up their own thoughts, manifest their own solutions, put down their electronic devices, get off the couch, get outside, and maybe even go to the Rocky Mountains and search for Fenn's treasure.

So, whether you are young or old or planning your first search or your hundredth, I believe everyone should enjoy "The Thrill of the Chase":

1. FORREST FENN'S BOOK.
and
2. WHEREVER YOUR SOLUTION TO FORREST FENN'S POEM TAKES YOU TO SEARCH FOR HIS TREASURE.

"In every walk with Nature one receives far more than he seeks."
John Muir

FLY FISHING
for GOLD

Searching for the end of Forrest Fenn's Rainbow
and his Treasure

By Jeff Uryjasz

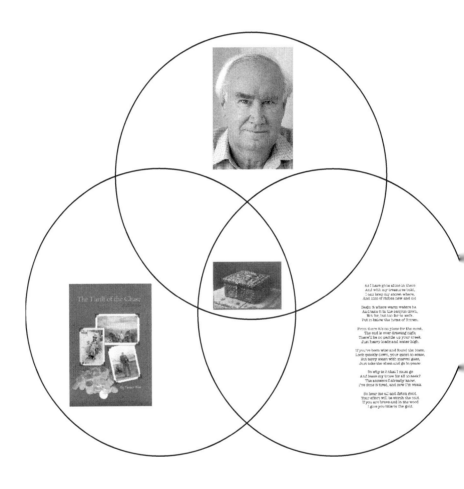

"It seems logical to me that a deep-thinking treasure searcher could use logic to determine an important clue to the location of the treasure. Is someone doing that now and I don't know it?" Forrest Fenn

Chapter 1:
THE "FENN" DIAGRAM

1. IF YOU ALREADY KNOW WHO FORREST FENN IS,
THEN BY ALL MEANS MOVE ON ALREADY.
and
2. IF YOU DON'T KNOW WHO FORREST FENN IS (or live
under a rock that happens to be located in the Rocky Mountains,
in which case, I highly suggest you "look quickly down" just to
be sure there is not a treasure chest hidden there), THEN GO
AHEAD AND TAKE A COUPLE MINUTES TO DO A QUICK
GOOGLE SEARCH. I will wait while you get overwhelmed with
an unbelievable number of search results that appear. Don't
worry, I get it…information overload. On top of that, you have to
sift through what's true, what's not, and an occasional comment
from a dolt. While I obviously don't know everything…LOL, I
have painstakingly compiled as much information as I could over
the years not only for myself, but also to provide in my book so I
come across as somewhat astute.

Now, I know if you're currently at this point, you have plenty
of questions. Who the heck is Forrest Fenn? Why did he hide a

treasure chest? Where do I look for it? What does the chest look like? What's inside the chest? Ok, slow down a little. Even though I will answer all those questions, I still believe you should purchase Fenn's memoirs and enjoy reading and learning more about him on your own. That being said, this section does contain everything you need to know about Forrest Fenn and his hidden treasure in a pinyon nut shell.

He was a commercial fishing guide around Yellowstone when he was young (in his early teens).

He has been an avid outdoorsman and fly fisherman his whole life.

He is a decorated United States Air Force fighter pilot who flew 328 missions in the Vietnam War and has also been shot down twice. He retired as a Major.

He searched, collected, and traded pre-historic artifacts for his art gallery. One of the artifacts he owns is Sitting Bull's peace pipe which is one of his prized possessions.

He currently lives in Santa Fe, New Mexico where he opened an art gallery, raised his family, continues to collect amazing artifacts, and write books.

Oh, that's right, how could I forget…
He hid a treasure chest.

When Fenn was diagnosed with kidney cancer in 1988, he decided to do the unthinkable. He was hell-bent on taking some of his wealth with him when he died. He gathered some of his treasures, secured them in a chest, and set a plan into motion to take that chest with him into the Rocky Mountains to a special and "secret" location where he was going to die with it (on his terms of course). But Fenn is a maverick, or more like a phoenix, who rose up and overcame the deadly grasp of cancer victoriously when it went into remission.

SO, WHAT DID HE DO?
1. He hid it anyway.
and
2. He wrote a book containing a poem with nine clues that if solved correctly would create a map with directions that if followed precisely would take someone to the end of his rainbow and the treasure chest.

SO, WHAT AM I GOING TO DO?
1. MENTALLY SOLVE THE CLUES IN FENN'S POEM.
and
2. PHYSICALLY GO FIND FENN'S TREASURE CHEST.

I gotta go…You finish up with the logistics and I will catch up with you later.

Forrest Fenn's Books

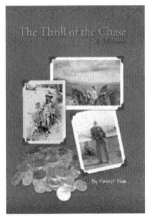

"The Thrill of the Chase" A Memoir
by Forrest Fenn
Published: Jan. 1st, 2010

"TTOTC" is Fenn's first memoir containing stories about his life and his hidden treasure. The book includes the poem which holds the clues to the treasures' location. Fenn also said the book has hints sprinkled throughout the chapters.

"too far to walk" by Forrest Fenn
Published: Sept. 1, 2013

"tftw" is Fenn's second memoir tells his tales of living along the edges as he includes more stories about his life and family. The book includes the treasure map.

"Once Upon A While" A Third Memoir by Forrest Fenn
Published: Nov 30, 2017

"OUAW" finishes the trilogy of Fenn's memoirs. It includes 39 more life stories and possibly more hints about his hidden treasure.

Other Research Material

"Some searchers overrate the complexity of the search. Knowing about head pressures, foot pounds, acre feet, bible verses, Latin, cubic inches, icons, fonts, charts, graphs, formulas, curved lines, magnetic variation, codes, depth meters, riddles, drones or ciphers, will not assist anyone to the treasure location, although those things have been offered as positive solutions. Excellent research materials are TTOTC, Google Earth, and/or a good map." FF

In "TTOTC", Fenn also mentions a few books that were really important to him when he was younger and possibly even more so to this day. I have read those books and I highly suggest you read them too because I found some interesting information that was helpful to my interpretations of the clues and my eventual solution to the poem. The following is a list containing a couple of those books along with the other research materials I have used.

"Flywater: Fly Fishing Rivers of the West"
by Grant McClintock

"Journal of a Trapper or Nine Years Residence among the Rocky Mountains Between the years of 1834 and 1843"
by Osborne Russell

Journals of the Louis and Clark Expedition

"Ramblings and Rumblings" Fenn's un-published history

Professional internet articles and interviews with Fenn

Google Earth...and a good map of the Rocky Mountains

Forrest Fenn's Poem and Map

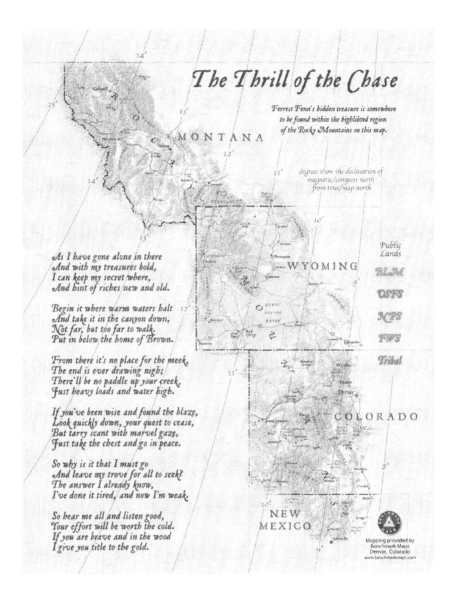

The Thrill of the Chase

Forrest Fenn's hidden treasure is somewhere
to be found within the highlighted region
of the Rocky Mountains on this map.

degrees show the declination of
magnetic/compass north
from true/map north

MONTANA

WYOMING

Public
Lands

BLM

USFS

NPS

FWS

Tribal

COLORADO

NEW
MEXICO

Mapping provided by
Benchmark Maps
Denver, Colorado
www.benchmarkmaps.com

As I have gone alone in there
And with my treasures bold,
I can keep my secret where,
And hint of riches new and old.

Begin it where warm waters halt
And take it in the canyon down,
Not far, but too far to walk.
Put in below the home of Brown.

From there it's no place for the meek,
The end is ever drawing nigh;
There'll be no paddle up your creek,
Just heavy loads and water high.

If you've been wise and found the blaze,
Look quickly down, your quest to cease,
But tarry scant with marvel gaze,
Just take the chest and go in peace.

So why is it that I must go
And leave my trove for all to seek?
The answer I already know,
I've done it tired, and now I'm weak.

So hear me all and listen good,
Your effort will be worth the cold.
If you are brave and in the wood
I give you title to the gold.

States and Land Designations

Fenn's treasure chest is hidden in the Rocky Mountains somewhere within the area shown in one of the four following states:

Montana
Wyoming
Colorado
New Mexico

Fenn's treasure chest is hidden on land with one of the following designations:

BLM - Bureau of Land Management
USFS - United States Forest Service
NPS - National Park Service
FWS - Fish and Wildlife Service
Tribal - Tribal and Indian Land

The legal ramifications of finding a hidden (or a buried) treasure varies greatly from area to area. I suggest you research the federal and state laws of the areas you are interested in searching. It is illegal to bring metal detectors or dig in most of those areas and depending on where you find it, you might have to turn it over to the local authorities (like a Park or Forest Ranger) unless you "go in peace" (quietly) that is. Some searchers believe that those legalities have influenced where Fenn has hidden the treasure. Fenn did spend a lot of money on a lawyer to find out the answers regarding those legalities, but I believe that he still hid the treasure chest where he wanted to anyway despite any laws, rules, or regulations. Now that would be a "bold" move indeed Mr. Fenn.

Forrest Fenn's Treasure Chest

What actually is Fenn's treasure chest?

The treasure chest, aptly named "Indulgence", is said to be an antique bronze Romanesque lock-box that dates back to around 1150 A.D.

How big is the treasure chest?

The chest is approximately 10" L x 10" W x 5" H and can hold about 600 cubic inches of treasure.

What does it weigh?

The filled chest is said to be around 42 lbs.

Fenn has said he over payed for the box because it was exactly what he was looking for. But Why? Most likely because of its size and also because the exterior is made of bronze. Upon exposure to air, bronze oxidizes, but only on its outer layer. This patina consists of copper oxide, which eventually becomes copper carbonate. The oxide layer protects the interior metal from further corrosion. In essence, bronze is resistant to corrosion. So, no matter where Fenn hid the treasure (either on land exposed to rain and snow or actually in the cooling waters of a river, stream, or creek), that would ensure the integrity and longevity of the chest. That's a good thing because Fenn even said it might not be found for a hundred or even a thousand years from now.

What's Inside the Chest?

Fenn has changed the contents of the chest multiple times over the years prior to the time he hid it, so there is not a lot of photographic evidence of the exact items currently in the chest.

The following is a list of the items known to be in "Indulgence".

- 265 gold coins, mostly American eagles and double eagles, and some Middle Eastern gold coins that date back to the 13th century.

- A little bottle of gold dust.

- A turquoise and silver row bracelet with 22 pre-historic beads in it.

Fenn has said this is the one item he regrets placing in the chest and he even offered to buy it back from the person who finds it. I would just give it back to him…wouldn't you?

- Hundreds of gold placer nuggets. Two of the nuggets are as large as hens' eggs and weigh more than a troy pound each.

- Gold dragon bracelet with ruby eyes and covered in diamonds.

- An unknown number of diamonds.

- Two gold frogs. They are very old and the larger frog is about 3" in length.

- Mayan gold beads.

- Eight emeralds.

- Gold turquoise necklace. Fenn excavated the pre-historic turquoise disc bead himself at San Lazaro Pueblo and had a goldsmith attach it to a gold nugget with an 18k gold post. The bead dates back to 1325 A.D. The nugget is approximately 1.75 inches long and is 2.105 troy ounces.

- Two Ceylon sapphires.

- A solid gold pre-Columbian nose ring.

- About 280 rubies.

- Two five-inch pre-Columbian gold mirrors.

- A Tairona and Sinu fetish necklace about 2,500 years old. The fetishes are made of carnelian and quartz crystal and semi-precious stones.

- Ancient Chinese carved jade figures.

- Pre-Columbian Wak'as.

- A 17th Century Spanish gold and emerald ring.

- A glass jar containing Fenn's 20,000-word autobiography and a couple of white hairs from his head. The lid has been dipped in wax to prevent moisture from getting inside.

There are also items Fenn has not discussed only to say that the finder will like the top two treasures when they open the chest.

What's it all worth?

ENOUGH. Since the price of gold rises and falls daily, the true value of the chest is unknown.

Is that Forrest Fenn fishing the Madison River next to a large rock that has a carving of the blaze of a horse? NOPE.

Chapter 2:
FAKES, FORGERIES, AND PHOTOSHOP

I want to take a brief moment to talk about how it pays to be extremely cautious navigating the internet in your search for information regarding Fenn and his treasure. No, I am not trying to question your nor anyone else's intelligence. It's just that it has been several years since Fenn's treasure hunt began and now there are way too many vlogs and websites out there solely dedicated to Fenn and his treasure. So many in fact, that the more I keep reading and searching online about Fenn and his treasure, the more I realize that the internet keeps getting littered with an over-abundance of photoshopped images, fake news, false information, and all sorts of other misinformation. I have found that some of Fenn's email responses, hints, and quips that these websites and their commenters have posted were not regurgitated precisely the way they were supposed to have been, you know, word for word. That could lead to an exponentially growing chain of mis-interpretation. Kind of like the old grapevine game where you would whisper into the ear of the person sitting next to you and then they would do the same to the person next to them and so on. By the time you got to the end of the line the information was almost always wrong. I hated that game. Maybe it was because grapes make me queasy.

On one occasion, during an interview I watched, I heard a respected woman news reporter ask Fenn what the house of brown was. I'm sorry, but there is definitely a difference between the "house of Brown" and the "home of Brown". DID SHE EVEN READ THE POEM? AARGH!

I also watched a video of two guys (allegedly stoned out of their minds) say they knew exactly where the treasure chest was, but didn't even realize until they drove out to West Yellowstone, Montana that Hebgen Lake was not even located in Yellowstone National Park. DID THEY EVEN LOOK AT A MAP? AARGH!

There are also several interesting, but misleading YouTube channels out there. One of them features a couple of searchers telling you where not to look…LOL. If they were smart enough to know all of the places the treasure chest is not, surely, they would have found it by now, right?

On another YouTube channel, a guy claimed to have already found the treasure chest, but he was not willing to provide any photographic evidence that proved he had it in his possession. For some strange reason his videos about Fenn's treasure are no longer posted. Weird huh?

It's misinterpretations like those that really stink because it requires new treasure searchers twice as much time to sift through all of that garbage just to determine whether or not the information that they find is accurate to begin with.

Then there are the internet photos. You know, the photoshopped ones that make you think you see something in the picture that really isn't there. Let it be known that there are no photographs on the internet that will aid you in finding Fenn's treasure, but since a few of the locations in some of these photos were actually located near my search area, I decided to take a little time to debunk them. Your welcome.

Is that Forrest Fenn fishing along the bank of the Madison River and looking over to view his treasure chest located "in", but not "under" the water?

NOPE.

Is that a painted black horse with a white "blaze" located near Fenn's "secret bathing spot" on the bank of the Firehole River at OJO Caliente Spring in Yellowstone National Park, Wyoming?

NOPE.

Now that you know

who Forrest Fenn is,

why he hid a treasure chest,

what you need in order to find it,

where you need to look,

what you need to look for,

and

what you need to avoid,

I know exactly where you are.

Chapter 3:
THE MEAT AND POTATOES

Ah, I knew you would be here. WELCOME. I hope you didn't skip directly to this chapter because you might have missed something really important. Naw, I'm just kidding. I actually placed everything of importance in this chapter for the sake of convenience. Now pull up a chair and get comfortable because this is where you're going to get fed all of the information regarding my thoughts about Fenn himself, his possible methods and writing style, my interpretations of his books, what I like to call "Fenn-isms" (quotes of Fenn's own words either written to searchers in cryptic email responses or possible hints spoken during interviews), my approach and solutions to his poem, and the story of my actual "BOTG" (boots on the ground) search for his treasure chest.

It is important to note that none of my solutions to the clues were forced. They all came organically through the aforementioned information and I tried to keep my solutions simple and logical because, well, that's what Fenn advised everyone to do.

*"Well I will give you a clue. Try to simplify if you can.
That's good advice." FF*

Also, you might notice that I am a little repetitive with some
of the information I provide in this chapter. It is mostly due to the
fact that my thoughts and solutions tend to overlap because of the
ways I have broken everything down. But, that's a good thing as
it reinforces the importance of some of those things.

Remember, all of the information in this book is purely and
simply my perspective. And, while you might not agree with me
on everything, like starting this sentence with the word "and",
maybe you will agree with me on just one thing in this book that
helps you complete your own solution to Fenn's poem and lock
down a location for your own "BOTG" treasure search. That is,
or course, if I have not already found the treasure.

Safety and the Search Area

*"It is **NOT** necessary to move large rocks or climb up or down a steep precipice." FF*

1. SAFETY.

As of this writing, many people have lost their lives looking for Fenn's treasure from either falling off of steep cliffs or in the fast-moving waters of a river. Don't try to be Indiana Jones. Remember, Fenn was almost 80 years old when he hid the treasure, he made two trips to his car due to the weight of the treasure, and did it all in one afternoon. He walked to it. He didn't climb, swim, or swing on a tree vine. He walked to it. Now, this does not mean that you do not have to possibly walk or wade across a shallow waterway. It is just a reminder that you have to be prepared based on your search area and take any necessary supplies with you if you are venturing into the mountains, forests, canyons, or rivers of the Rocky Mountains. Proper clothing (possibly even waders), a GPS, a sandwich, water, a flashlight, bear spray, bug spray, and maybe even a bed roll. Remember the number one rule…SAFETY FIRST.

2. THE SEARCH AREA.

If you truly listen closely to the things Fenn has said since hiding his treasure, you will see that he is not only telling you something, but ultimately guiding you, if just slightly, in the right direction. By telling searchers that they don't need to move large rocks or climb up or down a steep precipice, not only is he telling everyone to be safe of course, but is also quietly saying that the overall elevation change of the search area is not that steep. It is just another tiny hint to add to the list of descriptive information of your search area. (Hint: You should be searching somewhere that is relatively flat.)

Fenn has done everything he could do to inform everyone about any possible dangers regarding the search area of his hidden treasure. The rest is up to you. So, whether you're going on your first search or your hundredth, please follow all of his advice. Don't go anywhere an 80-year-old man couldn't go, don't go out searching the mountains when it's cold and there is snow on the ground, be cautious of the dangerous wildlife, and do not take any unnecessary risks to reach your search spot. If it's either extremely far or difficult to get to…the treasure chest is not going to be there.

North American Brown bear (aka grizzly bear)

"Grizzly bears alone are something to think about." FF

The grizzly bear, or more commonly known as the Brown bear, is a large population of bear that inhabits North America.

During an interview on ABC Nightline titled "Deadly Treasure" that aired on January 12, 2018, Fenn said that, *"Grizzly bears alone are something to think about."* When the interviewer goes on to ask Fenn if he had anything else to add, Fenn says that he has already said too much. I believe he really did say too much because that grizzly bear statement is a potential game-changer for many searchers. There are two key elements to this statement that need to be discussed.

1. SAFETY.

Fenn's statement is reiterating the fact that everyone must be alert and aware of not only grizzly bears alone, but all of the dangerous wildlife that live in the wilderness. This area is their home, their habitat, and we must respect that. Keep your eyes peeled, be cautious, don't get to close to them, and watch your back. STAY SAFE.

2. THE SEARCH AREA.

But there is also a deeper meaning to his statement. Fenn saying that grizzly bears are something to think about is his way of straight-up telling everyone that there are actually grizzly bears roaming around the area his treasure chest is hidden. That is extremely important in regards to the search area. (Hint: Search somewhere that has a population of grizzly bears.)

Not many states have a current population of grizzly bears. And since the search area is confined to the only four states; Montana, Wyoming, Colorado, and New Mexico, I had to research which of those states hold true to Fenn's statement. So...

Where are the grizzly bears?

■ ■ ■ *Post-glacial*
■ ■ *Historic*
■ *Present*

Photo Credit: Cephas from Wikimedia Commons,
The free media repository.

The above map shows the shrinking distribution of the grizzly bear during post-glacial, historic, and present time. When looking at the present time designated by the dark brown color, it can be seen that the current population of grizzly bears occurs in only two of the four states included in the search area (Montana and Wyoming). Not only would this eliminate Colorado and New Mexico as potential states to search, but it would increase the overall odds to a 50/50 chance of looking in the correct state.

To support the information depicted on the above map, I also found an article from June 27, 2014 titled "Trail Dust: Grizzlies, greatly feared once roamed New Mexico mountains" written by

Marc Simmons. He goes on to note that at one time grizzlies were fairly common in New Mexico, Arizona, and southern Colorado, but over the years, hunters, ranchers, and bounty hunters were to blame for the plummeting population. Here is a timeline showing that declining population.

1918 – Only 60 grizzlies remained in the Southwest
1928 – The U.S. Forest Service estimated the count at 28 grizzlies in the national forests of the area.
1936 – The U.S. Forest Service updates the count to only 10 grizzlies left.

After the early 1940's, there were no known sightings of grizzly bears in New Mexico or Arizona and they were thought to be extinct. In fact, the article even notes that if they wanted to re-populate New Mexico with grizzlies they would have to get them from Yellowstone National Park. Interesting huh?

1979 - The last grizzly bear located in southern Colorado was killed after it had attacked and seriously injured a wilderness guide.

Even though these key pieces of information have helped me reduce my search area down to two states (Montana and Wyoming), I still want to point out a few other facts about all four of the states associated with the search area that have contributed to my decision to eliminate them.

Then I will be able to use these facts along with the information I researched from other material to narrow down the search area to just one state. Stay tuned.

Montana

MONTANA is a popular choice for many searchers (including myself) as the location of Fenn's hidden treasure for many reasons. Here are a few interesting facts that might reinforce your thoughts regarding this state as well.

Montana is also known as "The Treasure State" because of its rich mineral reserves. That would make it kind of fitting considering we are looking for a hidden treasure filled with gold and jewels.

The town of West Yellowstone is in Gallatin County, Montana and also there is a portion of Montana that lies within the boundaries of Yellowstone National Park. This means that the treasure chest could be considered both in Yellowstone and in Montana at the same time. Even in the preface of Fenn's second book "tftw", he tells a story about fishing in that part of the park in Montana along a portion of the Madison River from a spot starting only a few miles east of the Yellowstone National Park entrance and continuing downstream to Bakers Hole. Fenn said that trip "cemented his connection" to that country. Oh yeah, that part of Montana is considered "Yellowstone Country" and their motto is "BOLDLY GO".

In my section on "Judging Fenn's Books by Their Covers" I show an interesting, but possibly just coincidental, detail about the cover of his first memoir showing the treasure having a possible connection to Montana.

Even Fenn's family is connected to Montana. Fenn's mother passed away near Cameron and his sister lives in Bozeman.

And let's not forget, there are grizzly bears in Montana.

Montana is definitely one of the states in my search area.

Wyoming

WYOMING is probably the number one choice for many searchers (again including myself) as the location of Fenn's hidden treasure. Why? How many reasons do you want? Well, here is a whole bunch.

What's in Fenn's chest? Gold. Yellowstone can also be considered a reference to gold because…well, gold is a yellow stone.

"Yellowstone is where my heart is." FF

"I absolutely loved that place." FF

Wyoming is the home to Yellowstone National Park. That is the place where Fenn spent every summer (June, July, and August) with his family camping and fishing until him and his siblings were grown. Don't forget he was also a fishing guide there in his early teens.

But, the connection doesn't just end there. Fenn has expressed his love for that place on more than a few occasions and even has a chapter in his book "TTOTC" titled "In Love with Yellowstone". Wouldn't you want to hide your treasure in a place that is near and dear to you? A place you love and are passionate about. If that that's not an endorsement, I don't know what is.

One other interesting thing is located in a book Fenn references in "TTOTC" called "Flywater". On page 72 in a chapter titled "Freestones", there is a caption that talks about the upper Yellowstone River and states that fishing there "Puts in perspective the National Treasure that is Yellowstone Park". So, wouldn't it be fitting if Fenn hid the treasure in Yellowstone National Park. That would make Fenn's treasure chest a "National Treasure". Right?

Actually, there are also a lot of searchers who think the opposite. They believe that Fenn would not talk as open or as much about Yellowstone National Park if he actually hid the treasure there. My answer to that is in the form of an old saying.

"If you want to hide something, hide it in plain sight."

Hiding the treasure chest in Yellowstone National Park and then writing about it in your book would be a great way to be both straightforward and somewhat misleading at the same time.

Another reason a lot of searchers don't think Fenn would hide the treasure there is due to the fact that your supposed to declare any findings (e.g. the treasure chest) to the Park Ranger. Well, that would still leave you with two options if you found it.

1. "Just take the chest and go in peace."
This line in Fenn's poem could be telling you that if you find the chest to just take it and leave quietly without anyone knowing about what you found and where you actually found it.

2. "I give you title to the gold."
If you find the chest you could go to the Park Ranger seeing as you legally have a right to keep the chest.
If Fenn is deceased when the treasure is found it would go to the finder or if Fenn is still living they would attempt to return it to him. But Fenn has already stated in the poem that if you find it, he "gives you title to the gold". He is basically giving the finder legal ownership whether he is living or not.

"Grizzly Bears alone are something to think about." FF

Again, this is an important statement, not only for the safety reasons I stated before, but also regarding the search location and it is also something I can personally substantiate. Since my solution to Fenn's poem led me to Yellowstone National Park,

Wyoming (home to over 600 grizzly bears which are also known as Brown bears…hmm "home of Brown"?), I decided to bring bear spray along with me…and I am glad I did. While I was lucky enough to encounter a large grizzly bear that came out of the woods directly across the Madison River from me during my "BOTG" search, I was fortunate enough that it was far enough away from me and didn't care enough to stick around as he tromped quickly back into the woods. I am just upset I didn't get to take a photographic proof before we both parted ways. I think I was too busy planning my escape.

Wyoming is definitely one of the states in my search area.

THE MEAT AND POTATOES

THE MEAT AND POTATOES

Colorado

COLORADO is one of the states I discarded from my search area fairly quickly. Nothing in Fenn's books jumped out at me and gave me the feeling he had a strong personal connection to Colorado.

Early searchers were quick to associate the Grand Canyon with the line in Fenn's poem, "And take it in the canyon down", but when Fenn talked about hiding the treasure, it took him two trips from his car to hide the treasure chest, and I highly doubt he went down into the Grand Canyon, came back up, went down again, and came back up at almost 80 years old…and in one afternoon to boot.

Searchers were also mesmerized by something Fenn's friend and author Douglas Preston wrote in the forward of Fenn's third book and memoir "Once Upon A While". He wrote about where he thinks Fenn's car would be found after his death. In the parking lot of the Denver Museum of Nature and Science. If Douglas Preston knew that much about Fenn, he would have already published a book about how he found the treasure chest.

And let's not forget about the fact that most of Colorado has no population of grizzly bears.

I believe the treasure chest is NOT in Colorado.

31

New Mexico

NEW MEXICO is another one of the states I have ruled out from my search area and I am going to pitch you a few of the very important reasons why.

The first reason is that Fenn currently lives in Santa Fe, New Mexico and has said the following about the chest.

"The treasure chest is full of gold and precious jewels and is more than 66,000 links north of Santa Fe." FF

Using my land surveying knowledge, I know the following; 100 links = 1 chain, 66,000 links/100 links = 660 chains, 1 chain = 66 feet, 660 chains = 43,560 feet, and 43,560 feet/5,280 feet = 8.25 miles. So, Fenn is telling everyone that the treasure chest is <u>more</u> than 8.25 miles north of Santa Fe, New Mexico.

But it does make me wonder why Fenn was so cryptic with this hint and why he did not just say 8.25 miles. Is the 8.25 number important and have some sort or connection to his poem? Did he just want to keep treasure seekers far enough away from his home? Could it be both?

EITHER WAY, THIS IS A GOOD REMINDER FOR EVERYONE TO RESPECT FORREST FENN AND HIS FAMILY. STAY AWAY FROM HIS HOME. THE TREASURE CHEST IS NOT THERE.

STRIKE ONE NEW MEXICO.

"The treasure chest is NOT near the Rio Grande River." FF

This statement is the second reason I have discarded New Mexico from my search area. Fenn came out and said that right after the unfortunate loss of one of the treasure searchers. That statement alone eliminated one of the main search areas of many treasure hunters and just gave them another reason to move their searching northward.

STRIKE TWO.

"Grizzly Bears alone are something to think about." FF

I know what your thinking. The grizzly bear statement again. But, for me, this was the final straw in eliminating New Mexico from my search area. After finding those charts and articles that discussed the fact that New Mexico's grizzly bear population is extinct, I think you know where I am going with this...

STRIKE THREE...YOUR OUT.

I believe the treasure chest is NOT in New Mexico.

Mother Nature

Someone once asked Fenn whether the clues in the poem will also withstand the test of time.

"I am guessing the clues will stand for centuries. That was one of my basic premises, but the treasure chest will fall victim to geological phenomena just like everything else. Who can predict earthquakes, floods, mudslides, fires, tornadoes and other factors?" Forrest Fenn

I believe that if you're going to hide a valuable treasure-trove somewhere in the wilderness, logic dictates that you would try to think of everything in regards to placing that treasure chest in a spot that would, at the very least, reduce the chances of anything happening to it.

So, I researched my search area to see what Mother Nature could throw my way. The first thing to note is that no matter where you go in the wilderness you cannot escape the possibility of forest fires and even Fenn said the chest, which is exposed to rain and snow, could be scorched by a forest fire. Trees…check.

But as I continued my research, I did find some interesting information. If you take a look at the two maps on the following page you will see that the area where I focused my search, which is a relatively flat portion of the Madison River located within Yellowstone National Park that flows from Madison Junction in Wyoming downstream to Hebgen Lake in Montana (circled in red), lies between the Hebgen Lake Earthquake Area and the Yellowstone Volcano Caldera. Convenient huh? It is also located upstream and above three dammed sections of the Madison River; Hebgen dam, Earthquake lake Dam (aka Gallatin National Forest Dam), and the Madison Dam at Ennis lake. Now, I'm not saying that searching this area eliminates earthquakes, volcanos,

mud slides or potential floods from the equation. What I am
saying is that it only strengthens my solution to be searching in a
location that is not directly on top of or in the path of some
of these phenomena.

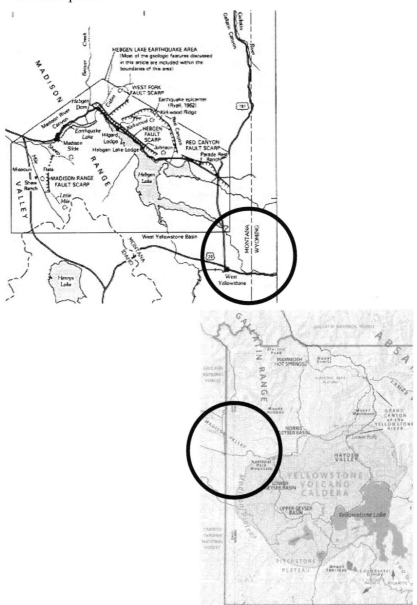

Search Area Fenn-isms

"It's at least 300 miles west of Toledo." FF

Fenn did a segment on the Today Show and they wanted him to continue giving hints every week. So, some of the hints including this one, were pretty generic and should just be taken at face value.

"The chest is hidden above 5,000 ft. and below 10,200 ft." FF

Good one Forrest. Most of the Rocky Mountains fall within that elevation range.

*"Where warm waters halt is **NOT** a dam." FF*

Thank you. I was getting tired of hearing about every new searcher starting their search at a dam, more specifically, the Hebgen dam.

"There isn't a human-trail in very close proximity to where I hid the treasure" FF

Well, this is a real vague one huh? This quote definitely could be taken two different ways.

1. There is not a human-trail <u>very</u> close, but there is one reasonably close to where Fenn hid the treasure.
2. There is not a human-trail very close, but there could be another type of trail very close. (e.g. game trail, horse trail, wagon trail)

"I made 2 trips from my car to the hiding place and it was done in one afternoon." FF

Fenn did say he made two trips because of the weight of the chest and the weight of its contents. That would mean he traveled

4x the distance from his car to the hiding spot in one afternoon which would imply that the distance is not that far.

"The spot is a secret and dear place, private...and I walked back to my car smiling. It's a very special place to me." FF

Again, I believe the spot where Fenn hid the treasure is not too far from where you can park. Maybe around 200 - 500 feet?

"Sure, I'm eccentric. I pride myself on being eccentric. I don't want to go down the center line like a lot of people do." FF

centerline:

1. a real or imaginary line through the center of something, especially one following an axis of symmetry.

I think Fenn might be hinting at the fact that he does not go down the centerline, but along the edges or banks of a river, stream, or creek.

"There are 654,885,389 acres of land in the United States that are owned by the American people. That is what the federal government admits is "public property." And the population of this great country is 313,914,040. After doing the math I learn that my allotment is exactly 2.086 acres. Now, what if I wanted to secret a can of Dr. Pepper under a rock in the cooling waters of a rivulet somewhere in my allotted public acreage?" FF

What an interesting quote or should I say analogy? What if Fenn wanted to "secret" (hide) an aluminum metal can of Dr. Pepper (or a bronze metal treasure chest) under a rock (under a rock "blaze") in the cooling (in the cold) waters of a rivulet (waters of a river, stream, or creek) somewhere in his allotted public acreage (on Public Land). Sound familiar?

Q: "Part of the area includes national parks, national forests, maybe Indian land. What have you figured out if the treasure is found in those areas? Who owns it?"

"This is not something I jumped into superficially, I mean, I tried to think of everything. My feeling is, if you can find the treasure chest you can have it." FF

Fenn put a lot of thought into the location of his hidden treasure including the land designations and respective rules and regulations regarding a find of that caliber.

Q: "But, if I find the treasure and it's in a national park, don't I have to share it with Uncle Sam?

"I spent a bunch of money with a lawyer to figure out the question about who owns it if it's found on public land, on private property, or on Indian land and there's all kind of answers. If it's found in a national park, according to my attorney, the person that finds it, is required to take it to the park superintendent and rules are different if you find it on private property. If you find it on Indian land, it really gets complicated." FF

Again, Fenn put a lot of thought into the location of his hidden treasure including the land designations and respective rules and regulations regarding a find of that caliber.

Q: "And the person who finds it has to deal with the legal questions?"

Well, if there is a legal question, yeah. What if there is not a legal question? My argument is the person who finds it is going to own it." FF

Fenn cannot reiterate enough that he put a lot of thought into the location of his hidden treasure including the land designations and respective rules and regulations regarding a find of that caliber.

Q: 2012 – What would Forrest personally still want to find?
There are so many bits of history I would like to find: a clovis point between the ribs of a mammoth, a letter written by my father to my mother before they were married, a special fishing spot on the Madison River that no one alive knows about but me." FF

Hmm…Fenn would like to find a special fishing spot on the Madison River that no one alive knows about but him. I guess there are others fishing at Fenn's "secret" fishing hole.

"If you have a searching partner, best to have them wait in the car." FF
1. Its not that far of a distance from where you park to the treasure chest.
2. You don't want anyone else knowing what you found and where you found it. Remember, two men can keep a secret if one of them is dead.

Q: So, no one is looking near the right spot?
"No one is looking at the right spot." FF

Searchers are getting close. Fenn has said that searchers have been "within" 200 feet of the treasure chest. Was I one of them?

"I've said in my book that the treasure is hidden in the Rocky Mountains north of Santa Fe – and I'm not going to tell the Indians it's not on Indian land, I'm not going to tell the Forest Service it's not on Forest Service land, I'm not going to tell some rancher out there it's not on his land – it's in the Rocky Mountains and I'm not going to narrow the search down." FF

Hmm…Did Fenn actually just narrow down the search area right to our face and tell us it's not on Indian Land, USFS Land, or Private Land? I think he did. which leaves us with BLM Land and National Park Service Land.

"Two men can keep a secret if one of them is dead." FF
1. Fenn is telling us not to share the "secret" location with anyone for your own safety.
2. I also believe Forrest is hinting at the fact that his father knew about his "secret" spot before his father died.

"My father had pancreas cancer. They gave him 6 months to live. 18 months later he was still fishing up in Yellowstone in those lakes and fast streams." FF

Before Fenn's father died, he made sure he saw Yellowstone one more time. He drove his father there, a distance of 1,700 miles one way, to where they camped and fished until all the Fenn children were grown. Yes, he said Yellowstone…not New Mexico or Colorado.

The Thrill of the "Chase"?

So, how did I begin my quest for hidden treasure? By reading and learning more about the man who actually hid it...Forrest Fenn. And where did I begin my analysis? His first memoir "The Thrill of the Chase" of course. It is the book that surrounds the infamous poem with the nine clues that need to be solved in order to construct the map that will provide directions that lead to the end of his rainbow and the treasure chest. Sounds easy huh?

Considering I already knew I was personally going to over analyze everything, including each and every word of the poem and their respective definitions, I figured that the title of Fenn's book would be an interesting place to begin since it's the first thing you read.

I already knew the word "Thrill" meant a sudden feeling of excitement and pleasure, which I was already feeling as I embarked upon this quest, but it was another word in the title that grabbed my attention. Upon further review of the word "Chase",

I noticed that it had two definitions that were both eerily relevant to Fenn's treasure hunt. Take a look.

Chase:
1. An earnest or frenzied seeking after something desired.
2. A tract (defined area) of unenclosed land used as a game preserve (An area of land where birds or animals are kept in protected conditions in the wild, either for conservation or to be hunted for sport).

The meaning behind the first definition is an easy one. That would be the thrill of searching for Forrest Fenn's hidden treasure chest. That's definitely something we all desire.

The second one is where things can get a little more involved. Ok, a lot more involved. You see, there are many so-called "chases" or defined areas of unenclosed land being used as game preserves within the Rocky Mountains. But, what area was near and dear to Forrest Fenn? Since, I didn't know that much about Fenn, I wanted and needed to find out more about his past, where he has travelled, what he enjoyed doing, and his thought process behind hiding a treasure and writing the poem in the first place.

So, I cracked open "The Thrill of the Chase" and read it straight through cover to cover. I really enjoyed his child-like perspective on his family and his life in general. He definitely had an adventurous spirit and a care-free attitude growing up. One thing I did immediately notice was his wit. Fenn begins his book with *"Well, I'm almost eighty"* and goes on to comment how funny it was to write it that way and that he could have just said he was seventy-nine. So...

almost 80 = 79 (or somewhere between 79 and 80)

I was going to just laugh it off as a funny little quip until a little further down the page Fenn wrote *"Actually, the only thing about me that's old is my body. My mind stays at about 13."* Since the word "almost" and "about" are synonyms I figured I could make the following assumption.

about 13 = 12 (or somewhere between 12 and 13)

Was this a hint to Fenn's mentality and thought process? Maybe. Was that a time in his life that holds his most dear and special memories? I don't know. What was he even doing when he was 12 to 13 years old? That I do know. After reading deeper into the book, I was greeted with the answer I was looking for. A full-page photo of Fenn with a bunch of fish he had just caught with the title "The Madison River" and the caption read, "A good day on the Madison River, I was twelve. What fish we couldn't use we traded for potatoes and other goods. It's what kept us going during the war when my father was making $4,000 a year teaching school in Texas." B-I-N-G-O! I felt I was starting to learn more about Fenn, his mentality, and his interests.

Ok...now where is the Madison River? The Madison River runs approximately 183 miles from where it begins in Yellowstone National Park, Wyoming at a place known as Madison Junction which is where the Gibbon River and Firehole River meet to form the Madison River to its confluence with the Jefferson and Gallatin Rivers near Three Forks, Montana. Got it.

Fenn goes on to write in a chapter titled "IN LOVE WITH YELLOWSTONE" that he spent every summer (June, July, and August) there with his family camping and fly-fishing in Yellowstone until every one of his siblings were grown. He even spoke very passionately about that place.

"I absolutely loved that place" FF

"It's where my heart is." FF

His affinity and passion for fly fishing doesn't end there. In another chapter in his book titled "FLYWATER" he discusses a few more interesting tid bits. He noted that the summers in Yellowstone seemed to pass so fast when he was a kid and he also reflects back to a time when he sat under a tree on the Madison River and wrote a note to his wife. Fenn even includes a cryptic photo in that chapter captioned "My secret fishing hole" which, without jumping ahead of myself, could offer some insight to one of the clues in his poem.

It is then he also talks about a different book coincidentally titled "Flywater" and how the color plates in that book were some of the places he used to fish as a kid with his father. Places he considered personal secrets. Places he considered to be his alone. And places where he guided others for pay when he was "just a young teen". A young teen…could that be thirteen?

Another interesting photo that pops up in Fenn's book is a full-page photo captioned "That's me at age thirteen, thinking about starting seventh grade." He later admits it was there at that age that his life really began. It is easy to see why Fenn's thoughts and memories revolve and revert back to between the ages of 12 to 13 years old. It was a very fun, important, special, and memorable time in his life.

Reading all of this definitely gave me some good insight into Fenn, his passions in life, and also as to some of the important locations where he spent most of his youth aside from school which is one of the reasons why I personally settled on Yellowstone National Park as my interpretation of the second definition of the word *"Chase"* Fenn is referring to in the title of his book and also a place of interest high up on my list in regards to where he might have hidden his treasure. That easily places me in portions of Montana and Wyoming and is also one of the reasons I eliminated Colorado and New Mexico from my search area.

So, what did I take away from the analysis of the title of Fenn's book? I learned that "The Thrill of the Chase" actually has two relevant meanings.

1. THE THRILL OF SEARCHING FOR FORREST FENN'S TREASURE CHEST.
and
2. THE THRILL OF EXPLORING THE WILDERNESS
(Or in my case, YELLOWSTONE NATIONAL PARK).

One other thing I find interesting and worth mentioning here is that I read somewhere that Fenn is a master of the "double entendre".

double entendre:
1. A figure of speech or a particular way of wording that is devised to be understood in either of two ways, having a double meaning. Typically, one meaning is obvious, given the context where, as the other may require more thought.
2. A word or phrase open to two interpretations, one of which is usually risqué or indecent.

Judging by Fenn's usage of the word "Chase" in the title of his book and his supposed penchant for the double entendre, I believe this is something to keep an eye on…or should I say BOTH eyes on because if the words in Fenn's poem lend themselves to multiple meanings, then maybe each of the clues in the poem also has to satisfy two meanings, in essence, creating a double solve. Just some more food for thought.

Judging Fenn's Books by Their Covers

They say, "Never judge a book by its cover", but with Forrest Fenn you just cannot dismiss them. So, I decided to take a deeper look at all three covers of his memoirs for any possible hints or clues.

The first thing I wanted to verify was…what exactly is a memoir?

memoir:
A reflection, or historical account, of one's own memories of certain events or people (Auto-biography) or written from personal knowledge of someone else (Biography).

A memoir is a reflection, huh?

Well, even though this has been pointed out by a few other searchers before, I feel that it would be wise to take another look at each of the covers of Fenn's three memoirs to see what the reflections of their images reveal.

"The Thrill of the Chase"

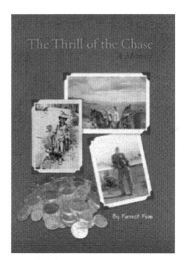

At first glance, there doesn't seem to be anything too revealing or out of the ordinary on the cover of "TTOTC". It just shows a few photos of Fenn during different times of his life that go hand-in-hand with the stories in the book and it also shows some gold coins which are part of the contents of his hidden treasure.

It is when you look at the reflected image of the book (or just turn it upside down) that you see something worth noting.

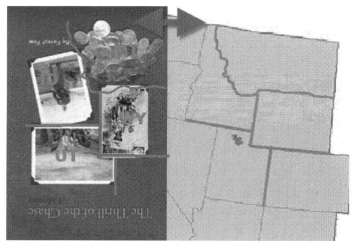

The layout of the photos on the cover appear to resemble a map of some of the states included in the treasures search area. More importantly, the photo of the gold treasure shown on the cover appears to be located in the state of Montana, which is also known as "The Treasure State". Is it just a coincidence?

"too far to walk"

What's interesting about the second book in Fenn's trilogy is that even though it is also a memoir of sorts, he does not call it a memoir on the cover. So, in this case, I decided not to look at its reflection, but to just examine the details of the cover and the cover photo itself.

The first thing I noticed about the cover of the book is that the title is NOT capitalized. It is written precisely like it appears in the line of Fenn's poem, "Not far, but too far to walk". But, not only does the title of the book reference the "too far to walk" clue, but jumping ahead a little to the books preface gives us more insight to it as well.

In the preface, Fenn recalls a story about a time he went fishing in the Madison River and walked downstream in the river from a spot a few miles from West Yellowstone Montana all the way to Bakers Hole. He goes on to say "The river distance was about 10 miles" and that for him now "it's too far to walk." Need I say more? Fenn has even referenced this fact by saying, *"If you read my preface, it doesn't take a genius, I think, to figure out what they're talking about."*

Next, I took a closer look at the cover photo. In the photo, Fenn appears to be wearing waders and holding a staff. A staff can be used for two purposes.

1. A WALKING STAFF. A walking staff is used for support in walking or hiking on land.
2. A WADING STAFF. A wading staff is used for support to wade out in a river with loose rocks on the bottom.

I believe Fenn not only uses the staff for walking or hiking along the banks of a river, stream, or creek, but that he also uses it to cross that waterway at the right spot, that is, once he has gone "too far to walk".

Also, in the cover photo we see Fenn's shadow being cast across the waters of a river, stream, or creek. In order for that to happen would mean one thing…the sun is behind him. In "TTOTC", Fenn talks about using what he called "mountain man wisdom" (which basically tells us that the sun rises in the east and sets in the west) which helped him determine his direction of travel. Fenn has also said he made two trips from his car to hide the treasure and he did it in one afternoon. So, if we take that into account along with the sun's location and its path of travel in the sky, I believe we can conclude that he walked or hiked along the south edge or bank of a river, stream, or creek.

This all leads me to believe that once you travel along a river into the canyon downstream a distance that's "too far to walk" (about 10 miles) you would then move on to the next clue in the poem which brings you that much closer to reaching the end of your quest. I will delve deeper into that hypothesis later in my actual breakdown of the poem and "BOTG" search.

"Once Upon A While"

What is interesting about Fenn's third memoir is that it was released a good deal of time after "TTOTC", "tftw" and his actual hiding of the treasure chest. Was it necessary for him to write a third memoir? Did Fenn feel it was needed as a way to covertly provide more hints? Well, after studying the cover very closely, it is indeed a possibility because there are a few things that stand out to me as possible hints.

The FIRST thing I noticed is that the stick figure Fenn drew in the cover art is fishing on one of the banks of a river and does not appear to be standing in the water. Could this drawing be a depiction of Fenn fishing at his "secret" fishing hole? Did he fish mostly from the bank or edge of a river? Is he hinting at which side of the river he fishes from?

The SECOND thing I noticed was a very faint, but visible white cross located directly behind that same stick figure. You can even see its reflection in the water below the title's text. Is this a reference to the "blaze"? Is that the cross and "x" that marks the spot of the end of Fenn's rainbow and the location of the treasure?

The THIRD and final thing I noticed on the cover was the image of some bright stars in the water where the stick figure is fishing. Since Fenn again titles his book as a memoir and the image of those stars are clearly a reflection of them from the night sky, I figured I would take a look at the reflection of this cover too. Yes…again I just turned the book upside down.

Not only does looking at the book this way reveal the way the stars would appear in the sky, but it also raises a few questions.

Does this view give us a better indication of the direction we are facing? Could the brightest star be the North Star and hinting at the possibly we should be looking toward the big northern sky? I mean, FYI, Montana is also known as "Big Sky Country".

Is that bright cluster of stars actually a constellation?

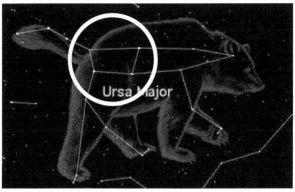

Is that constellation actually Ursa Major (also known as the Great Bear) in the night sky?

Is Fenn hinting at the direction of the river that is located at his "secret" fishing hole and also as to which side of the river he fishes from?

Or is all this just coincidental? Again, just more food for thought.

Important Literature

First Grade

No Place for Biddies

Jump-Starting the Learning Curve

Bessie and Me

My Spanish Toy Factory

Me in the Middle

Surviving Myself

Gypsy Magic

In Love with Yellowstone

The Totem Café Caper

My Brother Being Skippy

The Long Ride Home

Looking for Louis and Clark

Buffalo Cowboys

Stout Hearted Men

My War for Me

Blue Jeans & Hush Puppies Again

Teachers with Ropes

Tea with Olga

Father on the Banco

Flywater

Gold and More

Dancing with the Millennium

Hints in the Chapter Titles?

Fenn said, "The chapters in my book have very subtle hints, but are not deliberately placed to aid the seeker." But, what about the chapter titles? I mean, readers often skip over the chapter titles of a book almost as quickly as the preface.

So, after successfully analyzing the title of Fenn's first memoir "TTOTC", it made me more aware of potential possibilities for locating hints and I definitely did not want to skip over anything, and I mean anything. That meant that I also wanted to take a closer look at the titles of all of the chapters in his book to examine the possibility of any hints hidden within the chapter titles of Fenn's book "The Thrill of the Chase".

Upon closer inspection I found a few chapter titles that stood out to me.

IN LOVE WITH **YELLOWSTONE**
Upon researching Fenn, it's easy to see his passion for Yellowstone and fly fishing it's lakes and streams. Take this chapter's title alone "In Love with Yellowstone". That's a pretty bold statement. You cannot get more straightforward then that.

But Fenn has written a whole lotta other things re-enforcing his strong connection to Yellowstone. The following are just a reminder of a few of the things he has said.

"I absolutely loved that place." FF

"It's "where my heart is" FF

Why would he want to hide the chest anywhere else?

Is Fenn indirectly hinting that the chest is hidden
IN YELLOWSTONE NATIONAL PARK?

FATHER **ON THE BANCO**

Interesting. Why did Fenn use the word "banco"? Why didn't he just use the word "bank". If it was to draw attention to it, it worked on me. I decided to look up a couple of the definitions for the word's "banco" and "bank" for reference. This is what I found.

Banco: A portion of the floodplain or channel of a river cut off and left dry by the shifting of its course.
Bank: The land alongside or sloping down to a river or lake.

Is Fenn is hinting that the chest is hidden somewhere ON THE BANK OF a river?

FLYWATER

The chapter FLYWATER is interesting to me for two reasons:

1. In this chapter Fenn discusses visiting his father and talking about their favorite fishing spots. He also talked about the months (June, July, and August) he spent IN YELLOWSTONE. He continues to reflect back on a memory of when he "sat under a tree on THE MADISON RIVER and watched the osprey dive for fish" as he wrote a note to his wife. This is also the chapter Fenn includes a photo of his own captioned "My secret fishing hole". Remember, one of the lines in Fenn's poem reads "I can keep <u>my secret </u>where".

2. The book *Flywater*.

In Fenn's book "The Thrill of the Chase", under his chapter titled FLYWATER, he mentions the book *Flywater*. He then talks about how he used to fish some of the places shown in the photos of that book as a young teen. Young teen, huh? Would that be <u>about</u> 13? Remember, in the opening paragraphs of his book "The Thrill of the Chase" Fenn talks about his age when he writes, *"The only thing about me that's old is my body. My mind stays at <u>about</u> 13"*. He also said at that age he guided other fishermen for pay. Is this one of the "riches" Fenn writes about in his poem?

He then goes on to say those places were *"personal secrets"* to him and even though fishermen now frequent those places he always thinks about them as his *"alone"* and that it was about "being there, in the tranquility and silence of *one's self"*. His alone and one's self, huh? Remember, Fenn did say in his poem that "he has gone *alone* in there".

This prompted me to take a good hard look at the book *Flywater*. One thing that stood out to me the most in that book is in a chapter coincidently titled FLYWATER. There I found a photo of a fly fisherman holding his rod, which is arcing from the trout fighting him on the other end, captioned "THE MADISON RIVER". It reads:

"To be suddenly connected through a rainbow arc of rod and run of line to something as purely wild as God's own trout produces astonishment at a cellular level and, at least for a moment, blurs the border between man and nature. It is a bond which renews itself time after time and is the addictive essence of the sport."

Of course, I noticed "THE MADISON RIVER" caption, but I also noticed a couple other interesting details.

First, is the line mentioning the "rainbow" arc of rod and run of line which is a fly-fishing reference that could be interpreted as a hint from Fenn regarding the meaning of the "end of his rainbow", which is part of a statement he wrote in his book "TTOTC" located immediately before the poem, and is also something I really need to investigate further.

Second, I believe that "God's own trout" is a reference to Brown trout and possibly even Fenn's "home of Brown".

Is Fenn is hinting to the fact that if you solve the nine clues in the poem and follow them exactly, they will lead you to the end of his rainbow (his "secret" fishing hole) which is also considered FLYWATER and possibly located on THE MADISON RIVER?

and what's hidden nearby?

GOLD AND MORE

Gold and more, is simply just another way that Fenn describes the multiple objects which are known to be the contents of his treasure chest. I also believe that gold and more is a reference to the "treasures" and "riches" in his poem? Either way, it is safe to say, Fenn is describing what you will find...THE TREASURE CHEST.

Could Fenn's chapter titles be indirectly hinting to where the treasure chest is?

IN YELLOWSTONE NATIONAL PARK
ON THE BANK OF
THE MADISON RIVER
IS THE TREASURE CHEST.

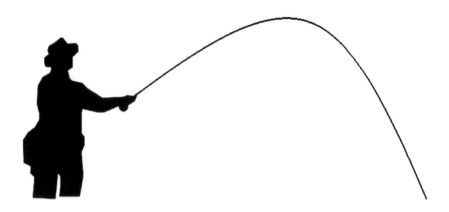

The Rainbow Connection: The end of Fenn's Rainbow

In the chapter titled GOLD AND MORE in Fenn's book "The Thrill of the Chase", located right before the poem, he wrote the following:

"So I wrote a poem containing nine clues that if followed precisely, will lead to the end of my rainbow and the treasure."
Forrest Fenn

Fenn basically states the fact that the poem has nine clues that if solved correctly will generate a map that provides directions, that if followed precisely (exactly), will lead you to the following two things:

1. THE END OF FENN'S RAINBOW.
and
2. THE TREASURE CHEST.

What could the end of Fenn's rainbow be?

"A physical rainbow arc of rod and run of line"

Once again, I bring up the book "Flywater", the book that Fenn references in his book "TTOTC". In the chapter of that book coincidentally titled FLYWATER, I found that photo of a fly fisherman holding his fishing rod, which is forming an arc from the trout fighting him on the other end. The photo, which is captioned "The Madison River", reads as follows:

"To be suddenly connected through a <u>rainbow arc of rod and run of line</u> to something as purely wild as God's own trout produces astonishment at a cellular level and, at least for a moment, blurs the border between man and nature. It is a bond which renews itself time after time and is the addictive essence of the sport."

A "rainbow arc of rod and run of line". What a beautiful way to describe fly-fishing. We already know that Fenn is an avid outdoorsman and fly fisherman who grew up camping and fishing in Yellowstone with his family until he and his siblings were grown and that he was also a fishing guide there in his early teens. Could Fenn be eluding to the physical arc created by his own fly-fishing rod and run of line to a special fishing spot, a spot he referred to in his book 'TTOTC" as "My Secret fishing hole"? And is Fenn's poem not only giving us directions to that "secret" fishing hole (also the special spot where he originally planned to die on his on terms), but also to where he hid his treasure chest? Well, it certainly appears that way to me.

But, of course, I believe there is more to it than just that. I believe that "the end of my rainbow" statement actually holds a couple deeper meanings and that they all hold true to Fenn and his poem. Let's take a look.

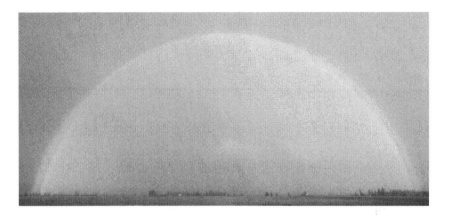

"An actual or theoretical rainbow?"

Rainbow:
A bow or arc of prismatic colors appearing in the heavens
opposite the sun and caused by the refraction and reflection of
the sun's rays in drops of rain.

While a real rainbow has no end as it is a circle of continuous light, it's some of the other facts about them that I found interesting.

1. Rainbows contact the ground at two points; a beginning and an end point. Those two points are also multi-directional as you can begin or end at either point.

2. You can theoretically draw an imaginary line connecting a rainbows two points and that line doesn't have to be a straight one to still maintain those two points (e.g. the line would meander if you are following along a river, a stream, a creek, a road, a path, or a trail).

3. Rainbows can be seen in the mist spray of a waterfall. Some treasure searchers believe that a waterfall is the "water high" Fenn is referring to in his poem and others are even looking for a real rainbow. I guess anything is possible.

Rainbows are also considered to be lucky, and traditional Irish stories often refer to a leprechaun hiding a "pot of gold" at the end of a rainbow.

"A metaphor for death?"

In many cultures a rainbow has been used as a metaphor for death. For example, the Buddhist tradition considers the rainbow to be the highest spiritual plane one can access before crossing over to the other side. Also, in some eastern cultures, a double rainbow is considered a symbol of transformation and is a sign of good fortune. The first arc represents the material world, and the second arc signifies the spiritual realm.

I believe one of the meanings regarding the end of Fenn's rainbow is a metaphor for death because he said that solving the nine clues to the poem will lead you to the end of his rainbow and the treasure which is also the place where he originally planned to die (on his own terms due to his then cancer diagnosis).

So, what is the end of Fenn's rainbow?

1. A PHYSICAL RAINBOW ARC CREATED BY HIS FLY-FISHING ROD AND RUN OF LINE TO A SPECIAL FISHING SPOT...OR WHAT FENN REFERS TO AS "MY SECRET FISHING HOLE".

2. A THEORETICAL (IMAGINARY) RAINBOW PRODUCED BY USING TWO POINTS (A BEGINNING AND END POINT) GENERATED BY SOLVING THE NINE CLUES OF FENN'S POEM/MAP AND FOLLOWING ALONG AN IMAGINARY LINE CREATED BETWEEN THOSE TWO POINTS TO HIS SECRET FISHING HOLE.

3. A METAPHOR FOR DEATH AND THE LOCATION OF FENN'S "BLAZE"; HIS PROSPECTIVE GRAVE SITE, GRAVE MARKER, OR GRAVE STONE (Seeing as he originally planned to die with his treasure chest at his "secret spot").

4. AN ACTUAL (REAL) RAINBOW? While it is actually somewhat feasible and not impossible, I would venture to say it is probably not a real rainbow.

And what will you find at the end of Fenn's rainbow? Well, fish of course, the "blaze", possibly Fenn's bones, and of course...

THE TREASURE CHEST.

It will take more than luck to find Fenn's treasure chest full of gold and more at the at the end of his physical, theoretical, and metaphorical, rainbow.

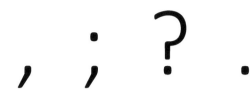

Punctuation:
The practice action or system of inserting points or other small marks into texts in order to aid interpretation; division of text into sentences, clauses, etc., by means of such marks.

Comma (,):
A comma indicates a pause between parts of a sentence. It is also used to separate items in a list.

Semicolon (;):
A semicolon or semi-colon separates major sentence elements. A semicolon can be used between two closely related independent clauses, provided they are not already joined by a coordinating conjunction. Semicolons can also be used in place of commas to separate items in a list, particularly when the elements of that list contain commas.

Question mark (?):
A question mark indicates a question. Also, it is used to express doubt or uncertainty about something.

Period (.):
A period at the end of a sentence designates a full stop. Terminate an idea, a phrase, or thought with finality and emphasis.

Punctuation in the poem.

Here I take a look at the importance of the punctuation marks used in the poem. So, let's first take a look at them individually to validate their usage.

Comma (,):
Fenn uses a lot of commas throughout his poem. I believe he did that along with the use of the word "and" on purpose as a way to limit his overall sentence count to a pre-determined number.

Semicolon (;):
Fenn uses only one semicolon in his poem. I believe he does this not only to keep his sentence count down, but also to provide two closely related statements that help validate not only each other, but also the description of your surroundings at that location.

Question mark (?):
Fenn uses only one question mark in his poem. Why is it that he is asking a question? To answer it of course. On the very next line he goes on to provide the answers (yes, two answers) to that very question. I believe he does this to help confirm his usage of double meanings, multiples, and plurals in the poem.

Period (.):
Since the poem is actually a map, I believe Fenn not only meant to mentally stop his thought or sentence at the period, but to physically stop at those points when following his directions. We'll see.

Do I believe that Fenn's use of punctuation marks follows the general rules of punctuation? ABSOLUTELY.

But, when he was asked about any further significance, he had this to say.

Q: Does punctuation have significance in solving the poem? If so, what?
"No." FF

No…How can this be? Fenn did say he felt like an architect when he constructed the poem and while the punctuation might not have significance to solving the poem, I believe it does have significance in creating a map along with the directions that that map provides.

Right after the line *"not far, but too far to walk."* not only did I notice the period (which would designate a full stop), but I also noticed that the next word Fenn uses, is the verb *"put"*, which is a word that performs an action. So, it appears to me that I go a specified distance and stop.

Then I am to perform the following action, *"put in below the home of Brown."* After *"put in below the home of Brown."* he writes *"From there…"*. Once again, the period stops you after you *"put in below the home of Brown"* and then you are given new directions *"From there"*.

Clearly you can see that the punctuation does have some other significance whether Fenn intended it to or not.

I believe Fenn uses punctuation marks along with the word "and" on purpose to limit his overall sentence count to a pre-determined number. Look what happens when you re-arrange Fenn's poem following the general rules of punctuation.

1. As I have gone alone in there and with my treasures bold, I can keep my secret where and hint of riches new and old.
2. Begin it where warm waters halt and take it in the canyon down, not far, but too far to walk.
3. Put in below the home of Brown.
4. From there it's no place for the meek, the end is ever drawing nigh; there'll be no paddle up your creek, just heavy loads and water high.
5. If you've been wise and found the blaze, look quickly down, your quest to cease, but tarry scant with marvel gaze, just take the chest and go in peace.
6. So why is it that I must go and leave my trove for all to seek?
7. The answers I already know, I've done it tired, and now I'm weak.
8. So hear me all and listen good, your effort will be worth the cold.
9. If you are brave and in the wood I give you title to the gold.

When you follow the rules of punctuation and re-arrange Fenn's poem into its complete sentences it reveals the following two things:

1. THE POEM CONTAINS **9** CLUES.
and
2. THE POEM CONTAINS **9** SENTENCES.

IS FENN HINTING THAT THE NUMBER **9** IS IMPORTANT?

As I have gone alone in there

And with my treasures bold,

I can keep my secret where,

And hint of riches new and old.

Begin it where warm waters halt

And take it in the canyon down,

Not far, but too far to walk.

Put in below the home of Brown.

From there it's no place for the meek,

The end is ever drawing nigh;

There'll be no paddle up your creek,

Just heavy loads and water high.

If you've been wise and found the blaze,

Look quickly down, your quest to cease,

But tarry scant with marvel gaze,

Just take the chest and go in peace.

So why is it that I must go

And leave my trove for all to seek?

The answers I already know,

I've done it tired, and now I'm weak.

So hear me all and listen good,

Your effort will be worth the cold.

If you are brave and in the wood

I give you title to the gold.

CAPITALIZATION in the poem

Q: Have the rules of capitalization been properly followed throughout the entire poem?
"Whose Rules?" FF

Here I examine the English rules of capitalization to see if Fenn has remained consistent throughout his poem.

First off, I noticed the first letter of each beginning word in all the lines of the poem are capitalized. This is somewhat normal because it is a traditional way of writing poetry. In other words, there's nothing to see here.

The only other word that is capitalized in the poem is the letter "B" in the word Brown. Fenn has highlighted this word for a specific reason, but the real question is, does it follow the standard rules of English capitalization for example, being a name or proper noun, or just does it follow Fenn's own rules just because of its extreme importance to him?

Some searchers think that Brown pertains to the Lamar Valley Ranger Station in Yellowstone National Park (Elev. = 6,565 ft.) being that it is the former home of Ranger Gary Brown. Home of Brown? But, since Fenn did say that structures of any kind are not involved, I have decided to discard that theory. Don't worry, that's ok, because the other two possibilities I have both fit perfectly into my solution.

1. BROWN TROUT. Brown trout is a no-brainer and is my personal choice as Fenn is an avid outdoorsman and fly fisherman. The home/habitat of Brown trout is in the water. And
2. BROWN BEAR. Brown bear is also known as a grizzly bear and remember Fenn said, *"Grizzly bears are something to think about"*. The home/habitat of Brown bear is the mountains.

As I have gone alone in there
And with my treasures bold,
I can keep my secret where,
And hint of riches new and old.

Begin it where warm waters halt
And take it in the canyon down,
Not far, but too far to walk.
Put in below the home of Brown.

From there it's no place for the meek,
The end is ever drawing nigh;
There'll be no paddle up your creek,
Just heavy loads and water high.

If you've been wise and found the blaze,
Look quickly down, your quest to cease,
But tarry scant with marvel gaze,
Just take the chest and go in peace.

So why is it that I must go
And leave my trove for all to seek?
The answers I already know,
I've done it tired, and now I'm weak.

So hear me all and listen good,
Your effort will be worth the cold.
If you are brave and in the wood
I give you title to the gold.

Forrest Fenn

Poem Fenn-isms

"Look at the poem as if it were a map, because it is, and like any other map, it will show you where to go if you follow its directions." FF

"All of the information you need to find the treasure is in the poem. The chapters in my book have very subtle hints but are not deliberately placed to aid the seeker. Good luck in the search." FF

With Fenn referencing important literature in his book "The Thrill of the Chase" along with providing titles to some of the books that are very important to him, I believe those books along with his own memoirs are more important than most people think, and I personally used information from all of them to complete my solutions to the poem clues.

"I've said it many times that everything about my poem and my book is straightforward." FF

straightforward:
1. Uncomplicated and easy to do of understand. Free from evasiveness or obscurity.
2. proceeding in a straight course or manner.

Here I believe Fenn means both definitions of the word "straightforward".

1. Fenn is saying that the poem is easy and uncomplicated to decipher. That is true to some extent because it is easy to look up the definitions of the words he uses in his poem and those words can only mean a couple things.

2. I also believe that the map the poem, or at least the first few clues of the poem, creates two points, and those two points form a line straight to "the end of his rainbow". Well, not exactly straight if it follows along a river, stream, or creek. In that case,

the line definitely would meander a bit. This so-called line could lead you to the end of Fenn's rainbow (his "secret" fishing hole) and the treasure would be hidden nearby. Maybe about 200 feet?

"Clues in consecutive order." FF

I see a lot of people jumping around, re-arranging the order of the clues, and even looking directly for the "blaze" first. Fenn said the clues are in consecutive order; so slow down, take one clue at a time, and if you don't have a clear path to the next clue, try again.

"Don't overcook my poem." FF

I believe Fenn actually means two things with this simple statement.

1. Don't overthink the clues. Think K.I.S.S. (keep it simple stupid).

2. Fenn was a decorated pilot in Vietnam and "overcook" is a term pilots often used in terms of locating a target. They might say "Don't overcook the target." which basically means don't go past your intended target. So, I think Fenn is hinting that the whole solution to the poem will not take you too far away from "where warm waters halt".

"Some folks correctly mentioned the first two clues to me in an email and then they went right past the other seven, not knowing that they had been so close." FF

Why would someone get the first two clues correct and blow by the rest of them? Simple, because they "overcooked" the poem. I believe that the third clue is the distance needed to travel to the next clue and that most people are misinterpreting that distance and are actually going right past Fenn's "secret" spot and the hidden treasure.

"If a person reads the poem over and over and are able to decipher the first few clues in the poem, they can find the treasure chest. It may not be easy, but it certainly isn't impo...I could go right straight to it." FF

Why would you be able to go right straight to the chest after solving the first few clues? Again, because I believe the third clue is the distance to the forth clue which would then, in turn, take you right straight to the location of the "blaze" and the hidden treasure.

Right:

1. Directional. On or to the right. (e.g. I could turn right, then go straight to it.)

2. In the exact location, position, or moment. Precisely. (e.g. I could go exactly to it.)

3. In a direct line, course, or manner. Directly. (e.g. I could go directly straight to it.)

"Read the clues in my poem over and over and study maps of the Rocky Mountains. Try to marry the two. The treasure is out there waiting for the person who can make all the lines cross in the right spot." FF

All the lines cross in the right spot huh? Again, I believe Fenn means both of the definitions of the word "cross".

1. I believe the lines of the map created by the poem will have you cross a river, stream, or creek in the correct location.

2. If you are smart enough to construct a map from the poem, then you yourself must physically cross that river, stream, or creek.

cross:

1. Go or extend across or to the other side of (A path, a road, a stretch of water, or area).

Physically walk/wade across a river, stream, or creek.

2. Pass in an opposite direction. (intersect, meet, join, connect)
If you have two lines on a map that cross in opposite directions, they can form an "X" at the point they intersect on a map. (→←)

3. A mark, object, or figure formed by two short intersecting lines or pieces (X or †).
If two lines cross perpendicular to each other, they form an "X" or a cross "†" on a map.

NOTE:
The letter "X" is the only letter of the alphabet NOT used in Fenn's poem.
Could an "X" or a cross "†" be the "blaze"? That would definitely satisfy two meanings and be something to consider.
1. An "X" marks the spot of the treasure on the map that the poem creates.
2. A cross "†" marks the spot of the end of Fenn's rainbow (grave marker) at the "secret" spot.

NOTE:
There is a drawing of a graveyard on the bottom of page 41 in Fenn's book "The Thrill of the Chase" that depicts a rotated cross that also looks like an "X".

"Searchers have been within 200 feet." FF
How does Fenn know someone has been within 200 feet? Well, it's because many searchers have emailed Fenn and told him exactly where they were. While he will not let anyone know they are "getting warmer", especially since "your effort will be worth the cold", I personally think that the "200 feet" is a significant number/distance and goes with my belief that the next clue takes you about 200 feet across a river, stream, or creek.

"Stop arm chairing that thing to death and get out there in the trees where the box is, but before you go, look at the poem as if it were a map, because it is, and like any other map, it will show you where to go if you follow its directions."
FF

Good advice. You have no chance of finding the treasure sitting at home behind a computer. Construct a map from the poem clues, get out there to the Rocky Mountains, and follow your maps directions to Fenn's treasure chest.

Q: Did the same 9 clues exist when you were a kid and to your estimation will they still exist in 100 years and 1000 years?
"The clues did not exist when I was a kid but most of the places the clues refer to did. I think they might still exist in 100 years but the geography probably will change before we reach the next millennia." FF

What? Most of the places the clues referred to existed. Not all of them?

"The person who finds the treasure will have studied the poem over and over, and thought, and analyzed and moved with confidence. Nothing about it will be accidental." FF
Do your homework and you can find the treasure.

"My guess is that the person who is successful will very quietly solve the clues and walk to the treasure with a smile on their face." FF

In Fenn's second book "to far too walk" he states he leisurely walked in the Madison River. So, just because he said the person who solves all the clues will walk to the treasure, doesn't mean they are not walking through the shallow waters of a river, stream, or creek.

The following is one of the more humorous questions Fenn was asked that somehow seemed to confuse many searchers.

Q: Can a little girl in India, who speaks good English, but only has your poem and a map of the US Rocky Mountains, work out where the treasure is?

"The little girl in India cannot get closer than the first two clues." FF

I believe the little girl from India could not get past the first two clues for two reasons.

1. The simple reason is because she is located in India and is not physically in the Rocky Mountains to do a "BOTG" search for the treasure.
and
2. She was referenced as only having the poem and a map, and I believe she actually needs Fenn's books, especially "too far to walk", to determine the third clue which is the distance that was provided in the preface of that book.

"Well I will give you a clue.
Try to simplify if you can.
That's good advice."
Forrest Fenn

"INDULGENCE"

"The chest is hidden in a safe but thrilling location." FF

Treasure Chest Fenn-isms

"What serious adventurers should remember is to not believe anything that is not in my poem or otherwise in my book. There's some misinformation out there. For instance, I never said I buried the chest, I said only that I hid it. That is not to say it is not buried." FF

buried:
1. *To put or hide under ground. Completely cover; cause to disappear or become inconspicuous. Hide, Conceal, Cover.*
hidden:
2. *To put or keep out of sight; Conceal from the view or notice of others. Conceal, Secret, Camouflage.*

"The chest is exposed to rain and snow and could be scorched in a forest fire." FF

scorch:
1. *To burn, char, or discolor the surface of something.*

So, no matter if the chest is slightly sunken into the ground or sitting "in" water, at least one of its sides is exposed to the elements.

"I know the treasure chest is wet." FF

Fenn has said that everything in the Rocky Mountains is wet regardless if it's "in" not "under" water or if it's 6 inches "in" not "under" the ground.

"The chest is NOT underwater." FF

underwater:
1. *Lying, growing, worn, performed, or operating below the surface of the water.*
2. *Being below the waterline of a ship.*

underwater vs. under water

Underwater is one word when it is an adjective preceding the noun it modifies. When it follows what it modifies, it is usually one word (e.g., the chest is not underwater), but underwater is still a fairly new compound (only about a century old) and is not 100% accepted, so some publishers still use under water when it follows what it modifies (e.g., the chest is not under water). This is becoming less common and you are safe with the one-word spelling for all uses of the word.

Remember, the treasure chest can still be considered "in" water, but not under water.

"The chest is unlocked and closed." FF

I would say the chest is somewhere secure enough to not be moved or tipped over very easily.

*"The chest is **NOT** in or related to a structure."* FF

No building, bridges, or dams are involved in the search.

*"The chest is **NOT** in a cave and **NOT** in a mine."* FF

Fenn has said that caves and mines are dangerous and have snakes and spiders in them. Remember, it's not hidden in a dangerous place.

*"The chest is **NOT** in a graveyard."* FF

No, Fenn did not hide nor bury the treasure chest in or near his father's grave nor anyone else's for that matter.

*"The chest is **NOT** under a man-made object."* FF

The "blaze" is a natural object like a boulder, rock, or tree. Most likely a boulder or rock as a tree would not stand the test of time due to; decay, a forest fire, etc.

"The chest is NOT in a tree, but is surrounded by trees...everything is surrounded by trees if you go out far enough." FF

I like this comment because, to me, it's very descriptive.

1. It's not inside a tree. Great news.

2. It is surrounded by trees, but everything is surrounded by trees if you back out far enough. I believe that the trees that surround the area of the chest are not that close because of another thing Fenn mentioned about the chest's location. Someone asked Fenn what he would see if he was standing where the chest was. One of his answers was "I'd see mountains". In my opinion, if there were trees surrounding the chest that were very close, you would only see those trees and not any mountains.

"And I told myself with my last gasping breath I was going to go out there and fling myself on top of that treasure chest and let my bones go back to the earth." FF

Gasp:

1. To catch the breath (as with surprise, shock, or pain).
What's funny to me is the example sentence that the dictionary provided. Example: He gasped as he stepped into the cold water.
2. to breathe with difficulty.
This just means that Fenn could either be standing on land or "in" the cold waters of a river, stream, or creek.

"Which is best, laying on the ground on a treasure chest, your bones rotting in the sun or laying in a hospital room with tubes down your throat." FF

This is an older quote, but an interesting one. Was Fenn just generalizing for the sake of the story he was telling?

"I think the gold will again become alert to the tromp and vibrations of hiking boots." FF

tromp:
1. To step hard.
vibrations:
1. A continuous slight shaking movement: A series of small fast movements back and forth or from side to side. A periodic motion of particles of an elastic body or medium in alternately opposite directions.

I guess this quote could pertain to either walking on land or walking "in" the water.

Q: You have mentioned sealing a bottle that is included in the chest with wax. What was your reason for doing this? Were you concerned merely for damp conditions or is the chest hidden in water?

"When I was ready to put the olive jar that contained my autobiography and two of my hairs in the treasure chest I studied the lid. It was made of tin coated steel, which is not easily oxidized in air and water. Over time those characteristics can break down. Although I am not ready to say the treasure is not in water, I certainly did not want moisture to enter the jar." FF

He is not ready to say the chest is not "in" water? What? I guess if it was that big of a safety risk he would have said something. I believe that there is water involved in the poem's solution, but that it's shallow enough to cross through it and also possibly shallow enough to have the chest sit "in" it.

Q: Are you willing to say whether the place of the treasure chest is the same as the one where you had previously plotted to have your bones rest forever?

"Yes, it is." FF

"The treasure is not hidden in a dangerous place in the normal definition of the word, realizing that there probably is no place on this planet that is safe under all conditions. Bloggers have quoted me as saying that a child could walk up to the treasure. I don't think that's an accurate quote because a three-year old girl would have a problem without some help. Remember, I was about 80 when I hid the chest, and had to make two trips." FF

A three-year old child would need help for two reasons.
1. Crossing even a shallow river, stream, or creek could throw you off balance or even cause you to fall because of the bed rock.
2. A three-year old child most likely would not be able to lift the 42 lb. chest.

"If I was standing where the treasure chest is, I'd see trees, I'd see mountains, I'd see animals, I'd smell wonderful smells of pine needles, sagebrush, and I know the treasure chest is wet." FF

Upon researching the area in Yellowstone National Park along the Madison River where I focused my search, I found information that resonated to me and mirrored the things Fenn says he sees at the chest's location. Some of the information describes the areas across the Madison River as an open sagebrush meadow backdropped by lodgepole pine forest and the mountains of the Gallatin Range and more specifically Mt. Holmes. That area was also a place to see Osprey, Bald Eagles, and waterfowl fly and swim through those waters. That sure sounds like most of the things Fenn sees around the treasure chests location to me. It also reminded me of the passage Fenn wrote in his book "TTOTC" about sitting under a tree on the Madison River watching an Osprey dive while he wrote a note to his wife.

The Copper Scroll

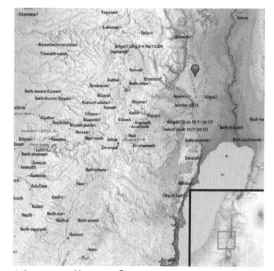

The Valley of Achor

The Ruin

Creating a Treasure Map from Written Text

Before I survey Fenn's poem, I will briefly examine how to dissect some simple written text to extract all the information needed to create a treasure map.

Using the Copper Scroll, which is part of the Dead Sea Scrolls found near Khirbet Qumran as my example, I will perform a quick walk through of the translated text line-by-line.

The following is an example of one of the English translations of the Copper Scroll's text.

1.1 In the ruin which is in the valley of Achor,
1.2 Under the steps leading to the East,
1.3 Forty long cubits: a chest of silver and its vessels
1.4 With a weight of seventeen talents.

The following is a list of the types of information I was able to extract from this example.
1. General location.
2. Specific location.
3. Beginning point or location.
4. Direction to next/end point or location.
5. Distance to travel.
6. Description of next/end location.
7. Distance to dig.
8. Description of what you will find.

The first line provides us with all the information regarding the main search area location.

1.1 In the ruin (2. Specific location and also our (3. Beginning location) which is in the valley of Achor, (1. General location)

The second line provides us with a direction to and description of the next, or in this case, end location.

1.2 Under the steps (6. Description of next/end location) leading to the East, (4. Direction to next/end point or location)

The third line provides us with the distance to dig under the steps.

1.3 Forty Long cubits (7. Distance to dig) 1 cubit was said to be 18 inches long which was based on the length of the arm from the elbow to the tip of the middle finger. Some cultures used 21 inches long. If we use 21 inches as the long cubit dimension, we get the following: 40 long cubits x 21 inches = 840 inches or 70 feet. That means you have to dig 70 feet under the East stairs.

The third line also provides us with a description of what you will find.

A chest of silver and its vessels (5. Description of what you will find)

The last line is just additional descriptive information on the chest and the vessels that you will find.

1.4 With a weight of seventeen talents (8. Description of what you will find) 1 talent = 965 troy ounces. 965 troy ounces x 17 talents = 16,396 troy ounces. 1 troy ounce = .0685 pounds. 16,396 troy ounces x .0685 pounds = 1,124.29 pounds.

So, if you go to the valley of Achor and find the ruin, go to the steps leading East and dig approximately 70 feet underneath the them and you will find a chest of silver and its containers weighing 1,124.29 lbs.

Congratulations!

My "BOTG"

Fenn's father once told him, *"Grab every banana...the train doesn't go by that banana tree but one time, so you reach out as far as you can, because every banana you don't grab is a banana you'll never have."*

OK. So, I have read a whole bunch of stuff; all three of Fenn's memoirs, Fenn's important literature, other reference materials, and every email and internet post of his I could find. I have also watched his numerous book signings and interviews. Then I analyzed every piece of information I compiled in every possible way that I could. What do I do next? I guess it is time to go and grab that banana.

Now it is time for you to come along with me on my actual "Boots On The Ground" quest for Fenn's treasure as I follow the directions to the map that my interpretation of his poem and my solutions to the clues created.

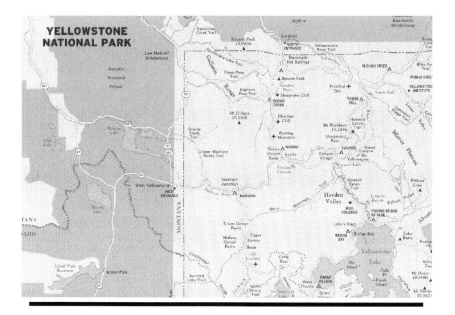

As I have gone alone in there

SPECIFIC PLACE WHERE FENN HAS GONE ALONE?

While we already know the general location of the chest is the Rocky Mountains, I believe Fenn uses his first stanza to hint at a more specific location.

AS
1. In the way that.
2. It's a fact that.

I (Forrest Fenn)

HAVE
1. used with a past participle to form the perfect, pluperfect, and future perfect tenses, and the conditional mood.

GONE (past tense)
1. Past participle of go.

ALONE (single, by himself)
1. Having no one else present.

IN
1. In or into.

THERE
1. That place or position.

While I don't know everywhere Fenn has ever gone alone, reading his books and the other reference material about him did give me some indication as to some of the places he did go alone.

Here are a few of those places that stood out to me and are not only are related, but also seem to hold a special meaning to Fenn.

Yellowstone National Park.
Fenn wrote about how he used to ride his bike "alone" into Yellowstone National Park "in there" to go to his "secret" bathing spot (OJO Caliente Spring located on the Firehole River).
He also wrote, on many occasions, about fishing "alone" along the portion of the Madison River that resides within Yellowstone National Parks boundary.

Madison River.
Fenn spoke about fishing "Nine Mile Hole", which is located on the Madison River, you guessed it, nine miles from the park entrance. He went on to say that that fishing hole only holds one fisherman. I guess that would mean he fished that spot "alone".

Also, in his book "too far to walk" he describes fishing *"alone"* as he walked in the Madison River from a spot a few miles from West Yellowstone all the way downstream to Baker's Hole.

Fenn even wrote about a time he sat under a tree "alone" on the Madison River and wrote a note to his wife.

So, not only has Fenn gone alone into the park, but he also gone alone into the Madison River to fish.

Firehole River.

As I said before, Fenn wrote about how he used to ride his bike "alone" into the park "in there" to go to the place he referred to as "my secret bathing spot" which is located near OJO Caliente Spring on the Firehole River.

So, not only has Fenn gone alone into the park, but he also gone alone into the Firehole River to bathe.

There are two different ways of looking at the first line of Fenn's poem.

1. AS (IN THE WAY THAT) I (FORREST FENN) HAVE GONE ALONE IN THERE.
and
2. AS (IT'S A FACT THAT) I (FORREST FENN) HAVE GONE ALONE IN THERE.

I believe that Fenn is utilizing BOTH. Not only is he telling everyone that it is a fact that he has gone alone in there, but also that his poem describes the actual way he has gone alone in there. That is, of course, if you have solved the nine clues in the poem correctly and follow the directions precisely.

I believe when Fenn is talking about going alone in there that it is in reference to:

1. YELLOWSTONE NATIONAL PARK.
and
2. THE MADISON RIVER.

And with my treasures bold,

SPECIFIC PLACE WHERE FENN HAS GONE ALONE AND WITH HIS TREASURES BOLDLY?

AND

WITH (plural)
1. accompanied by (another person or thing).

MY

TREASURES
1. A quantity or collection of precious metals, gems, and/or other valuable objects.

The noun "treasure" can be countable or uncountable. In more general, commonly used, contexts, the plural form will also be "treasure". However, in more specific contexts, the plural can also be "treasures". In reference to various types of "treasures" or a collection of "treasures".

In Fenn's Book "The Thrill of the Chase" he titles a chapter "Gold and More". Could this be an indication of the plural form of "treasures"?

1. GOLD (gold coins and nuggets).
and
2. MORE (precious jewels and artifacts).
or
1. THE TREASURE CHEST.
and
2. HIS FAMILY JEWELS (remember he did bathe naked).

BOLD
1. Courageous, confident, and fearless; ready to take risks.
2. Not hesitating to break the rules of propriety (rightness or justness; the conventional standards of proper behavior; manners, not modest.)

1. NOT HESITATING TO BREAK THE RULES. FEARLESS.
and
2. NOT MODEST (Again, he did bathe naked).

So, Fenn not only went "alone in there", but also with his treasures bold. Did he take his *"treasures"* into Yellowstone National park *"bold"* (fearlessly and not hesitating to break the parks rules)? I think so.

I believe Fenn not only went "alone", but also with his treasure chest boldly into:
1. YELLOWSTONE NATIONAL PARK.
and
2. THE MADISON RIVER.

I can keep my secret where,

PLACE WHERE HE CAN KEEP HIS "SECRET"

WHERE
1. In or at (what place) or position.

I (Forrest Fenn)

CAN
1. Be able to.
2. Be permitted to.

KEEP
1. Retain knowledge or possession of.

MY

SECRET
1. Kept from knowledge or view (hidden).

The noun "secret" can be countable or uncountable. In more general, commonly used, contexts, the plural form will also be "secret". However, in more specific contexts, the plural can also be "secrets". In reference to various types of "secrets" or a collection of "secrets".

WHERE I (FORREST FENN) CAN KEEP (RETAIN POSSESSION OF) MY SECRET.

I feel that the key word in this line is keep. It has to be a secret place that Fenn has not said or written anything about in regards to its location because talking about a secret place and telling you precisely where that secret place is are two completely different things.

Here's what I think…

My secret fishing hole

Photo credit: "The Thrill of the Chase" by Forrest Fenn

"My secret fishing hole" ☑

Idiom:
A phrase or an expression that has a figurative, or sometimes literal, meaning.

There is an old English Idiom "A picture is worth 1,000 words". I believe that about sums it up here. In the chapter titled "FLYWATER" on page 124 of Fenn's book "TTOTC", he provides a photo showing a lot of fish swimming in the water at an undisclosed location and it is captioned "My Secret fishing hole". It is the only place in his book that he uses the phrase "My Secret".

In that same chapter, Fenn goes on to talk about an important book to him coincidentally titled "Flywater" and about how he used to fish some of the places (depicted in its photos) as a kid and guide others for pay when he was a young teen. He considered them "personal secrets" that are now overrun with other fisherman even though he always thought of that space as his "alone". It sure looks to me like his fishing hole is a place he wants to "keep" secret, but it's also a good time to point out that just because it's a "secret" place to Fenn, it does not mean others have not been there.

I believe that what Fenn's refers to as "my secret" in his poem is actually two things.
1. FENN'S SECRET FISHING HOLE.
and
2. FENN'S HIDDEN TREASURE.

"So I wrote a poem containing nine clues that if followed precisely, will lead to the end of my rainbow and the treasure."
Forrest Fenn

As you can see, Fenn's two secrets also mirror the two things I believe the poem will lead you to if you follow its clues precisely.
1. THE END OF FENN'S RAINBOW (FENN'S SECRET FISHING HOLE).
and
2. FENN'S HIDDEN TREASURE.

But just to be fair, Fenn has written about a few other places that he described using the words "top secret", "my secret", and "secret" that are noteworthy. So, let's take a look at those.

"TOP SECRET"?

Top secret:
of the highest secrecy; highly confidential.

In Fenn's unpublished work "Ramblings and Rumblings: The Fenn History (unedited)", he discloses a few of his family's favorite fishing spots along the Madison River in Yellowstone National Park and he uses parentheses and all capital letters in the words "TOP SECRET" to describe those spots. Now, the average person might overlook "top secret" as just simply meaning that those places were important to him, but a man with a distinguished military background like Fenn would not. To a man like Fenn, those spots would be of the highest secrecy and highly confidential. He would definitely want to "keep" those places secret. Could one of those spots be the infamous "My Secret fishing spot" in Fenn's photo?

"The Slow Bend" – A productive section of the Madison River in both spring and fall as it holds both resident and migratory

Brown and Rainbow trout. It is located along side Riverside Drive, adjacent to a large riffle where the river flows only a few inches deep, which is about five miles up the river from the park entrance and coincidentally is nine miles from Madison Junction where the Madison's origin (beginning) is where the Gibbon and Firehole Rivers, both heavily heated by runoff from thermal areas, halt (end).

"Nine Mile Hole" – Which is appropriately named as it is nine miles from the park's west entrance. Remember, this spot is interesting because Fenn said it could hold only one fisherman. That could be a place he has "gone alone".

"Water Hole" – Which is about 11 miles from the park entrance.

After coming across this very interesting information, I realized that it actually helped me strengthen and solidify my solution to Fenn's poem and my search area even more.

WHY?

Because I found out that my search area is actually considered one of Fenn's "TOP SECRET" and highly confidential fishing spots. "The Slow Bend", which is a productive section of the Madison River (being that it is the "home of Brown" trout) is also located nine miles from Madison Junction, which is, coincidentally, my "Begin it where warm waters halt".

OJO Caliente Spring, Yellowstone National Park, Wyoming

"My Secret" bathing spot

There are several searchers that believe Fenn's "my secret" bathing spot has something to do with the poem. In a Blog written by Forrest Fenn in 2011 titled "River Bathing is Best", he goes on to describe OJO Caliente Spring. It is a hot spring (with a temperature of approximately 201° F or 94° C) in the Lower Geyser Basin of Yellowstone National Park and it is located a few yards off Fountain Flats Freight Road on the northern bank of the Firehole River and sits at an elevation of 7,182 feet.

Here I will point out the similarities of Fenn's Blog to the words used in the lines of his poem.

"Occasionally I'd ride my bike ("alone") *into Yellowstone Park* ("in there") *to a spot about twenty miles from town where a seldom-used dirt road turned right off the main drag. From there it was about a mile down that road to the Firehole River. Just before the river, there on the right, was*

a green geyser pool which spilled and spewed a small streamlet of boiling water that ran downhill for about fifty feet and into the cold ("cold") river. My secret ("My Secret") bathing spot, where the hot water tumbled into the stream was maybe four feet deep ("water high"?), and long, beautifully-green river grasses swayed back and forth in the gentle river currents just several feet distant. Sometimes I'd pull up a handful of grass and use it as a wash cloth. I never used soap there because I was afraid it was bad for my karma to pollute the pristine river.

I could change the water temperature ("warm waters"?) around my body just by moving a foot or so. Sometimes I stayed in that place for two hours or more and when I decided it was time to leave, I'd back a couple of feet downstream where the water was cold ("where warm waters halt"?) That gave me instant incentive to climb out and sun-dry in the tall grass that populated the river bank. It was a wonderfully uncivilized pleasure in a remote area where nothing could interrupt the purity of my naked (family jewels - "treasures") solitude ("alone").

I made that bike ride ("alone") more than a few times, even though it was somewhat arduous to pedal that far at only one manpower. But it was always worth the effort ("The effort will be worth the cold"?).

Now the National Park Service forbids swimming where geyser rivulets enter a stream. They also closed that little road to all vehicles, even though where it meets the river is one of the most beautiful places in the park, as buffalo and elk graze nearby and river otters often wiggle through the water looking for fish.

Several years ago, with my daughter Kelly's family, my wife and I drove to the little road (It's paved now) and walked to the river. I tried to get my granddaughters to swim where I had spent so many peaceful hours. The idea didn't interest them much. That spot, which was so important to me sixty-six years ago, is mostly overlooked now by the occasional passerby. My memories of those experiences are so dear to me that I hope in time all of my grandchildren will follow my footprints to that special place.

There is something about nude-dipping ("bold" - not modest, naked) in a mountain stream that awakens the fantasy of unfettered freedom lying restless just below the skin of all dreamers with romantic notions of the past, when life was roomier and less encumbered by the rules of social custom. Sometimes, when Kelly curls her long blond hair through her fingers in the sunlight, I am reminded of those long water grasses gently weaving and twisting in the river. Winters are cold for those without such memories. Surely, God underestimated his ability when he created the Firehole River."

Fenn has gone alone in the Firehole River to swim and bathe naked. That's pretty bold (not modest) and also (fearless, not caring about any park rules).

Getting back to the line in Fenn's poem "I can keep my secret where". I believe Fenn does not keep his secret here because he does not retain the knowledge of this location as he blatantly gives you directions and distances to the exact spot.

Is telling someone exactly where your secret spot is a good way to "keep" a secret. Absolutely NOT.

"Secret" family gear hiding spot

In Fenn's unpublished work "Ramblings and Rumblings: The Fenn History (unedited)", he briefly talks about his family's *"secret"* location near where they camped in West Yellowstone where they would hide their gear while they were away.

"We would just drive the car out into the forest about a half a mile and unloaded everything". FF

He goes on to say that their gear was always there when they returned. While that might seem like a great spot to put the treasure chest, it just does not feel right for two reasons. The first one is that Fenn only describes this spot as his family's "secret" location and not "My Secret" location. The second reason is that this information wasn't made readily available in any of his three memoirs. So, while you might be lucky enough to find something still placed there from the Fenn family, I don't think it will be Fenn's treasure chest.

Photo Credit: "The Thrill of the Chase" by Forrest Fenn

And hint of riches new and old.

WHAT'S AT FENN'S "SECRET" SPOT?

AND

HINT

OF

RICHES
1. MATERIAL WEALTH = Fenn's treasure.
and
2. VALUABLE NATURAL RESOURCES = Fish.

I believe valuable natural resources represents fish of course. In "TTOTC" Fenn, on multiple occasions, tells us of these valuable resources. On one account, in his chapter titled "FLYWATER" Fenn talks about guiding other people for pay when he was a young teen and, on another page, Fenn provides a full-page photo with the caption "Madison River" and it reads "A good day on the river, I was twelve. What fish we couldn't use we traded for potatoes and other goods. It's what kept us going during the war..." That definitely sounds like valuable natural resources to me and, by the looks of the photo Fenn provides captioned "My secret fishing spot", the fish are plentiful.

NEW AND OLD
1. NEW RICHES.
and
2. OLD RICHES.

Fenn has given us the answers as to the types of "riches" (plural) we will find at his secret spot.

Material wealth and valuable natural resources can both be considered "New" and "Old" riches.

1. AND HINT OF RICHES (<u>MATERIAL WEALTH</u> - THE TREASURES IN THE CHEST) BOTH NEW AND OLD.
and
2. AND HINT OF RICHES (<u>VALUABLE NATURAL RESOURCES</u> - FISH) BOTH NEW AND OLD.

Begin it where warm waters halt

STARTING POINT/PLACE AND INSTRUCTIONS

BEGIN

1. Start; perform or undergo the first part of (an action or activity).

Thinking like a surveyor, this would be the point of beginning. This signifies the beginning of the directions at a specific point/place which from there will lead me to the end of Fenn's rainbow and his treasure.

IT

1. Used to refer to (a thing) previously mentioned.

2. Used to refer to (a thing) easily identified.

What is "it"? "it" has to be something you can begin. The two things I believe "it" represents are:

1. YOUR QUEST (journey).

And

2. A RIVER (stream or creek). Possibly the Madison River or the Firehole River.

WHERE

1. In or at what place or position.

WARM

1. Of or at a fairly or comfortably high temperature.
Possibly cold waters heated by geothermal features (such as hot springs).

WATERS

The noun "water" can be countable or uncountable. In more general, commonly used, contexts, the plural form will also be "water". However, in more specific contexts, the plural can also be "waters". In reference to various types of "waters" or a collection of "waters".
1. Flowing water, or waters moving in waves. A body of water such as a river.
Example: The warm waters of the Firehole River.
2. waters (plural) – Multiple rivers?
Example: The Gibbon River and the Firehole River are warm waters.

HALT

1. To bring or come to an abrupt stop. (cease, end, stand still)
2. A suspension of movement or progress, typically a temporary one. (to pause)
NOTE:
A river can halt at many different locations. Here are a few examples.
1. the confluence or source of another river.
Example: The Madison River "begins" at Madison Junction where both the Gibbon and the Firehole Rivers halt (stop, end, cease).

2. A lake or reservoir.
Example: Hebgen Lake at an elevation of around 6,000 feet is considered to be a premier Stillwater fishing lake and popular recreational reservoir in Montana. The waters of the Madison River halt at Hebgen Lake.

3. A dam.
Of course, a dam halts water, but remember Fenn has already said, "WWWH is not a dam". So, using this information I have eliminated a few lakes in the area as a potential "WWWH" due to the fact they would not exist without their dams not to mention it would be a potential flood threat to a treasure chest hidden below a dam. Those lakes I excluded are: Hebgen Lake, Earthquake Lake, and Ennis Lake.

So…
I have a general location…The Rocky Mountains.
I have my specific location…Yellowstone National Park.

And now…
I believe I have my starting point/place…Madison Junction.

After researching Fenn, and reading "TTOTC", I decided to start where the Madison River begins and the warm waters of the Gibbon River and Firehole River end at Madison Junction. But, you see, a river has two edges and I have to be more specific because Fenn said something interesting in an email response to a searcher.

"Sure, I'm eccentric. I pride myself on being eccentric. I don't want to go down the center line like a lot of people do." FF
I believe Fenn is hinting at the fact that:
1. He doesn't like to do things the same way other people do. and

2. He doesn't travel down the actual centerline, of say, a river, and that he prefers to walk along the edges.

Fenn has also commented on "WWWH" by saying:

"If you don't have that one nailed down you might as well stay home and play Canasta." FF

And since everyone knows that a nail hits at a specific point (kind of like a dart hitting a bullseye), I am not just beginning at Madison Junction, but more specifically, the point where the Firehole River meets the Madison River. This is not only because of its location (which is along the South edge of the river), but also due to the fact that Fenn has a history with the Firehole River and used to bathe in its warm waters alone and naked (with his family jewels out there for the whole world to see). Remember, like I said earlier, The Firehole River is one of the places I know of that Fenn has "gone alone and with his treasures bold". If that isn't a double entendre, I don't know what is.

1. BEGIN (START) IT (<u>YOUR QUEST</u>) WHERE WARM WATERS (THE <u>GIBBON AND FIREHOLE</u> RIVERS) HALT (STOP) = MADISON JUNCTION.
And
2. BEGIN (START) IT (<u>A RIVER</u> - THE MADISON RIVER) WHERE WARM WATERS (THE <u>GIBBON AND FIREHOLE</u> RIVERS) HALT (STOP) = MADISON JUNCTION.

And take it in the canyon down,

INSTRUCTIONS AND DIRECTION TO TRAVEL

AND

TAKE
1. AS A MEANS OF TRANSPORTATION.
and
2. AS A MEANS OF PROGRESSION.

IT
1. Used to refer to (a thing) previously mentioned.
2. Used to refer to (a thing) easily identified.
    What is "it"? Now "it" has to be something you can both begin and take in the canyon down (a specific direction). The two things I still believe "it" represents here are:
1. YOUR QUEST (journey).
and

2. A RIVER (stream or creek). Possibly the Madison River or the Firehole River.

IN
1. In or into.

THE

CANYON
1. A deep gorge, typically one with a river flowing through it.
2. A deep narrow valley with steep sides and often with a stream flowing through it.
NOTE: The Madison River and the meadow located around Madison Junction lie in the broad Madison <u>Canyon</u>.

DOWN
1. Downstream.
2. Below or in a lower position or elevation.
3. Southerly direction (South).

1. AND TAKE (<u>AS A MEANS OF TRANSPORTATION - PHYSICALLY</u>) IT (YOUR QUEST AND THE MADISON RIVER) INTO THE CANYON DOWN (DOWNSTREAM AND A LOWER ELEVATION).
and
2. AND TAKE (<u>AS A MEANS OF PROGRESSION</u> – BOTH MENTALLY) IT (YOUR QUEST AND THE MADISON RIVER) INTO THE CANYON DOWN (DOWNSTREAM AND A LOWER ELEVATION).

Not far, but too far to walk.

DISTANCE TO TRAVEL FROM WWWH (THEN STOP?)

If you read my preface, it doesn't take a genius, I think, to figure out what they're talking about." FF

Here is an excerpt from the preface of Fenn's second book aptly titled and also noticeable uncapitalized "too far to walk":

"I put a small rubber dingy in the Madison River a few miles from West Yellowstone Montana and fished downstream to Bakers Hole. That part of the river was in the quietly forgotten western edge of Yellowstone Park. There were no roads, no trails, and no rangers to tell me I wasn't supposed to do that. The river distance was about 10 miles and the best fishing was in the bends were the water turned greenish deep and beautiful. The small boat containing my camping gear was tethered to my belt as I leisurely walked in the quiet river. I spent 3 days there casually casting my fly and enjoying the solitude. The river experience cemented my connection to that special country and I promised myself that someday I would make that trip again. That day never came for me and my disappointment still casts a lonesome shadow across the Madison River. **For me now it's too far to walk.**"

Fenn says that the river distance was about 10 miles and for him now it's too far to walk. Remember at the beginning of my book I said the way Fenn wrote about his age was important? Well, this is why I stressed its importance. Again, he uses the word "about" which as we already discussed earlier is a synonym for the word "almost". That leads me to believe I can conclude the following:

about 10 = 9 (or somewhere between 9 and 10)

This would give me a river distance of between 9 and 10 miles.

Another thing I observed was Fenn' usage of a period at the end of this sentence, and as I stated in my section "Punctuation in the poem.", I believe it was completely intentional.

Period (.):
A period at the end of a sentence designates a full stop. Terminate an idea, a phrase, or thought with finality and emphasis.

Since I know that the poem is actually a map, I believe that Fenn uses the period at the end of this sentence to both:

1. MENTALLY STOP HIS THOUGHT OR SENTENCE IN THE POEM.
and
2. TO TELL US TO PHYSICALLY STOP AFTER TRAVELING THE DISTANCE REQUIRED.

The following is the two meanings I extrapolated from the "too far to walk" clue.

1. THE DISTANCE REALLY IS NOT FAR, JUST TOO FAR TO FULLY WALK IT AND IT IS EASIER IF YOU TAKE ALTERNATIVE TRANSPORTATION SUCH AS A CAR, A RUBBER DINGY, OR MAYBE YOU CAN EVEN BORROW FENN'S BICYCLE.
and
2. GO A RIVER DISTANCE OF 9 MILES PRECISELY (OR SOMEWHERE BETWEEN 9 TO 10 MILES) AND STOP.

Since the distance is "too far to walk", I started at Madison Junction and drove my rented car on the main road that is located on the north side of the Madison River and follows the river downstream into Madison Canyon. I went a distance of about 10 river miles and then parked so I could walk along the bank of the river from that point. Also, I figured that if I needed to, I could work my way back upstream to explore more of my search area if needed.

One interesting thing I noticed was that since I began my quest and the Madison River at Madison Junction, it didn't matter whether I walked along the south bank (or edge) of the Madison River or drove in a car on the road that follows along the north bank (or edge) of the river, I would still end up in the exact same location. How? That is because the main road actually crosses over the Madison River at Seven Mile Bridge and then continues to follow along the river on the south side. I guess it doesn't matter that it was "too far to walk" and I drove there because I ended up at the same location anyway...Standing on the south bank of the Madison River with the sun to my back casting my lonesome shadow across a little part of the 200 feet of river in front of me flowing from right to left as I started looking for the "blaze".

Put in below the home of Brown.

INSTRUCTIONS THEN (STOP)

PUT
1. Enter, go, set foot, penetrate, proceed.

IN
1. Used as a function word to indicate, location, or position within limits.

PUT IN
1. To launch a small boat. (nautical) Example: The kayakers put in below the dam.

BELOW
1. In or to a lower place or elevation.
2. Underneath; Beneath.
3. Beneath the surface of the water.
4. Downstream.

5. South of.

There are also some interesting excerpts from some of the books Fenn referenced in "TTOTC" in regards to the word "below".

"Journal of a Trapper" by Osbourne Russell
1. "encamped on a stream running into the river about 12 miles *below* the fort, called Port Neuf."
2. "This valley commences about 90 miles *below* the Soda Springs, the river running west of South Rocks…"
3. "We went with them to the camp we found about 10 miles *below*."

"Journals of the Louis and Clark Expedition"
1. "Arrived at Bruno's Island 3 miles *below* halted a few minutes."
2. "I halted at this place being about 15 miles *below* Mussel Shell River."
3. "We encamped on Stinking River about 15 miles *below* the Forks…"

THE

HOME
1. Place where one lives permanently.
2. The native habitat for (animals)

OF

BROWN
1. BROWN TROUT.
and
2. BROWN BEAR

. (PERIOD) (STOP)

115

Here I believe Fenn's instructions are telling you to:

1. ENTER IN BENEATH THE SURFACE OF THE WATER OF THE RIVER WHICH IS THE HOME OF BROWN TROUT.
and
2. ENTER IN BENEATH THE SURFACE OF THE WATER SOUTH OF THE MOUNTAINS WHICH IS THE HOME OF BROWN BEAR.

I stepped foot into the Madison River, but I didn't just enter the water anywhere. You will just have to continue reading to understand why.

"Many go fishing all their lives without knowing
that it is not fish they are after."
Henry David Thoreau

From there it's no place for the meek,

DESCRIPTION (LITERAL & FIGURATIVE)

FROM

THERE
1. That place or position.

IT'S
1. It is.

NO
1. Not any.

PLACE

FOR

THE

MEEK
1. Weak.
2. Modest, Timid, Shy.
3. Religious meaning. Matthew 5:5 – "Blessed are the meek: for they shall inherit the earth."

"Some searchers overrate the complexity of the search. Knowing about head pressures, foot pounds, acre feet, bible verses, Latin, cubic inches, icons, fonts, charts, graphs, formulas, curved lines, magnetic variation, codes, depth meters, riddles, drones or ciphers, will not assist anyone to the treasure location, although those things have been offered as positive solutions." FF

Fenn said above that there are several things you don't need to have knowledge about in order to solve the clues, but that those things have offered positive solutions. I believe that bible verses are one of those things because if the meek shall inherit the earth, then no place for them means you are in the water.

1. (LITERALLY) FROM THERE (THAT PLACE OR POSITION YOU ARE CURRENTLY AT) IT IS NO PLACE FOR THE MEEK (A WEAK PERSON TO WALK OR WADE).
and
2. (LITERALLY AND FIGURATIVELY) FROM THERE (THAT PLACE OR POSITION YOU ARE CURRENTLY AT) IS NO PLACE FOR THE MEEK (YOU ARE WALKING OR WADING IN THE WATER).

So, I proceeded to walk across the Madison River in search of the "blaze".

The end is ever drawing nigh;

DESCRIPTION (LITERAL AND FIGURATIVE)
AND CAN BE DIRECTIONAL

THE

END

IS

EVER
1. At all times; always. Constantly. Continually.

DRAWING NIGH
1. Drawing near. Coming closer. Approaching.
2. Gently guide or pull (someone or something) to the left.

1. (LITERALLY) THE END (OF YOUR QUEST) IS EVER (CONTINUALLY) DRAWING NIGH (DRAWING NEAR - GETTING CLOSER).

2. (LITERALLY AND DIRECTIONAL) THE END IS EVER (CONTINUALLY) DRAWING NIGH (GUIDING OR PULLING YOU TO THE LEFT).

3. (LITERALLY AND FIGUATIVELY) THE END (OF YOUR LIFE) IS EVER (CONTINUALLY) DRAWING NIGH (DRAWING NEAR - GETTING CLOSER).

Wait, a metaphor for death? Hold on. Don't get frightened. Yes, we all will literally die someday, but there is no need to die right now looking for the chest if you proceed with caution and keep your search area somewhere relatively safe.

But, from Fenn's perspective, on the other hand, this metaphor was to become literal much sooner as he did say he originally planned on dying with the treasure chest (on his own terms due to him having cancer at the time).

At this moment, I know (and feel) I am literally getting closer to the "blaze" (and my own mortality) as I ford the Madison River and its heavy loads continued to literally pull me to the left as its strong current flowed downstream from my right to my left. But I continued on.

I also remembered what I said earlier about Fenn's use of a semicolon at this point in his poem. It means that the following two lines of the poem should mirror these previous two lines and reinforce the description of my current location.

There'll be no paddle up your creek,

DESCRIPTION (LITERAL AND FIGURATIVE)
AND CAN BE DIRECTIONAL

THERE'LL
1. THERE WILL (future tense)

BE

NO
1. Not any.

PADDLE

UP
1. Northerly direction
2. Toa place perceived as a higher level
3. Upstream

YOUR

1. Of or relating to one or oneself. (Possessive)

CREEK

1. A stream, brook, or minor tributary of a river.

2. An inlet in a shoreline, a channel in a marsh, or another narrow, sheltered waterway.

One thing I found interesting upon researching the Madison River is that it has been said that most of the Madison River inside Yellowstone National Park resembles a large spring <u>creek</u> and has been called the world's largest chalk stream.

1. (LITERALLY) YOU ARE UP A CREEK (STANDING OR WALKING IN THE RIVER) WITH NO PADDLE.

2. (DIRECTIONAL)

a. (LITERALLY) YOU ARE WALKING IN A CREEK (RIVER) IN A NORTHERLY DIRECTION (ACROSS IT)

b. (LITERALLY) YOU ARE WALKING UP (UPSTREAM) A CREEK (RIVER) EITHER IN THE WATER OR ALONG ITS BANK.

3. (FIGURATIVELY) YOU ARE UP A CREEK WITHOUT A PADDLE. YOU ARE (IN HOT WATER OR A DIFFICULT SITUATION WITH NO SIMPLE SOLUTION.)

There I was, "<u>no place for the meek</u>", walking northerly across the Madison River wishing I had a boat and a paddle (even though there are no boats allowed in this section of the river). Knowing I was in a difficult situation, I only stopped briefly to take a couple photos of my beautiful surroundings. Now where is that "blaze"?

Just heavy loads and water high

DESCRIPTION (LITERAL & FIGURATIVE)

JUST

1. Only.

HEAVY LOADS

1. Multiple lodgepole pine trees.

Fenn said he used to work for a logging company. Those type of companies usually refer to transporting a large group of trees as "heavy loads".

2. River loads.

a. The waters current.

b. Most rivers flow quickly in the steeply sloping sections near their source. Fast moving water washes away gravel, sand and mud leaving a rocky bottom. Fast moving water can carry lots of sediment as **bed load** and **suspended load**. Slower moving water can't carry as much when a river slows down.

Heavy rocks are dropped first, followed by gravel and then sand. Gravel and sand are dragged, rolled and bounced along the bottom of the river is called the **bed load**. Finer sand and mud that is supported by the water column is called the **suspended load**. Some minerals are dissolved in the water. These minerals form the river's **solution load**.

AND

WATER HIGH
1. Deep water.
2. A waterfall. (Note: A waterfall can create a real rainbow in the mist.)

Someone once asked Fenn about the possibility of someone finding his car parked near his spot and he replied, *"What is wrong with me just riding my bike out there and throwing it in the **water high** when I am through with it?"*

Also, here is an excerpt from "Journal of a Trapper" by Russell Osborne. "The snow melting raises the **water** so **high**."

JUST (ONLY) HEAVY (RIVER) LOADS AND WATER HIGH (DEEP WATER THAT RUNS HIGH UP MY LEGS).

I continued walking in a northerly direction across the Madison River as its strong current was "ever drawing nigh". I could literally feel the heavy loads of the river on my legs and under my feet as well as see how deep it was in front of me as its waters continued to flow downstream from my right to my left.

These last two lines of the poem did indeed mirror the two previous lines. They also seemed to verify my current location and I knew I must be close to finding the "blaze".

125

If you've been wise and found the blaze,

END POINT/PLACE

IF

YOU'VE
1. YOU HAVE (past and present tense)

BEEN (past participle of be)

WISE
1. Smart. Having or showing wisdom or knowledge usually from learning or experiencing many things. Based on good reasoning or information. Showing good sense or sound judgement.
2. Spiritual.
3. A wise Owl? Maybe because an owl is completely aware of its surroundings, has the ability to look 270° around, and possess keen vision. That would definitely come in handy when looking for a "blaze".

126

AND

FOUND (past participle of find)

THE

BLAZE

WHAT IS A BLAZE? Well, let's first look at what a "blaze" is as it is defined in the dictionary.

1. A trail marker.
The most common types of trail markings are called blazes, a term that can also refer to trail markings in general. You'll find two main types of blazes out on a trail; **painted blazes**, which are symbols painted on trees or rocks and **carved blazes**, which are chiseled into trees or rocks on the side of a path. Coloration can vary from location to location, but standard blazes are usually marked in white paint.

2. A usually white spot or stripe down the center of an animal face.
Example: a broad white stripe running the length of a horse's face.

3. An intensely burning fire.

There are also many ideas from other searchers that ranged from the above examples to some of the following: An "X" or a cross "†", double omegas, a totem pole, an arrowhead, the side of a bluff, a waterfall, a rainbow, and even a live owl in a tree.
While we can define the host of things a "blaze" can be, it is figuring out which one is the important one Fenn uses. The following quotes are things Fenn has said about the "blaze".

"blaze" Fenn-isms

"The blaze is a physical thing. It's not theoretical. Boy, did I
give you a big clue. That's not a clue. I mean, it doesn't take
a scientist to figure out a blaze is something you can look at."
FF

Q: What is Blaze?
"Anything that stands out." FF

Q: Is the blaze a single object?
"In a word...Yes." FF

Q: I would like to know if the blaze can be seen during the day
without a flashlight?
"I would say yes." FF

"I was careful, a blaze can be on a tree, in a fire, on the face
of a horse, and a host of others." FF

"A horse has a blaze on his forehead here. I mean, rocks have
a white face that could be a blaze. I mean, there's a fire
that's blazing. I mean, I could give you a thousand different
scenarios there, and all of them come to me by email.
Everybody finds a different one. The fact is, the important
one is out there." FF

"What does the word 'blaze' in the poem mean? A horse can
have a blaze on its forehead, a blaze can be scraped on a tree
to mark one's way, a blaze can mean a flame, or a scar on a
rock." FF

"If you find the correct starting point and follow the poem to the blaze, you will find the treasure chest. The treasure is at the blaze, if you follow the correct first clue. The blaze cannot be seen from Google Earth." FF

Q: Mr. Fenn: How far is the chest located from the blaze?
"I did not take the measurement, but logic tells me that if you don't know where the blaze is it really doesn't matter. If you can find the blaze though, the answer to your question will be obvious. Does that help?" FF

"Rocking chair ideas can lead one to the first few clues, but a physical presence is needed to complete the solve. Google Earth cannot help with the last clue." FF

"While it's not impossible to remove the blaze, it isn't feasible to try, and I am certain it's still there." FF

"I mean, there's people driving down the street looking for a blaze, because that's one of the clues, but you can't start in the middle of the poem and find the treasure, I don't think, I mean, it would be a miracle if someone did." FF

So, now that we know what a "blaze" can be and even what Fenn has to say about his "blaze", let's take a look at several of those possibilities and determine their strengths and weaknesses in regards to; fitting into the poem, plausibility, longevity, and even the feasibility of removing it from its location.

The "blaze" can't be on a tree...can it?

One definition of a "blaze" is something carved or painted on a tree, and while Fenn has acknowledged that fact, he also has gone on to say that the chest is not in a tree, but is surrounded by trees and that everything is surrounded by trees if you go out far enough. That still leaves some searchers to believe that the chest is hidden under, or should I say, next to a tree.

A tree does lend itself as the proper canvas to host several of the symbols we can associate with Fenn's "blaze".

1. A carving or painting of an "X" or a cross "†".

2. A carving or painting of the blaze on a horse's head.

3. A carving or painting of Double Omegas.

4. A carving or painting of a "wise" owl.

Some searchers have associated the "if you've been wise" as not only being smart and spiritual, but possibly that the "blaze" is a live owl up in a tree standing sentinel over Fenn's treasure chest. I mean, you have probably heard the saying, "wise as an owl". And, even though owls are not really that wise, the owl has been regarded as wise all the way back to Greek and Roman mythologies.

A live owl…come on…It is not stagnant. It flies around, and not only that, it also has a life-span far shorter than the hundreds to thousands of years that Fenn said it might take to find his treasure.

But what if the "blaze" is an image of an owl? Possibly, a carving, a painting, or even a natural scar, of an owl on a tree.

Let's take a look at a good visual example.

If you look at the above left photo, you see a charred sentinel pine tree with what appears to look like an image of a sentinel owl (circled in red) on it. I also provided a photo of a real owl on the right for reference.

Why is this important? Because this exact tree stands (or should I say did stand) along the south bank of the Madison River in Yellowstone National Park. It could have been construed to hold some sort of connection to the line in Fenn's poem, "If you've been wise and found the blaze". Maybe if you are "wise" like an owl and found an image of an owl (the "blaze"), you can look down and find the treasure chest sitting there, concealed of course, right next to the tree.

Since this tree was located not far from my search area, I decided to go and check it out.

There it was, uprooted, lying on the ground decaying away. Clearly this tree was not going to stand the test of time...

And yes, I still did take a look around there for Fenn's treasure chest anyway.

So, while trees, especially many types of pine trees, can enjoy a long life-span, they also have to endure many dangers that threaten their longevity such as; forest fires, being chopped or knocked down, natural decay, and early death.

That is why I do not believe the "blaze" is on a tree.

Photo credit: "The Thrill of the Chase" by Forrest Fenn

A white spot/stripe down the face of a horse?

Now, hold on. I know what your thinking. It cannot be on a horse because it's a live animal and we already discussed the live wise owl shenanigans. But it still leaves us with the possibility of a carved or painted horse on a large rock. I mean, the blaze down the face of a horse could also be construed as radial pointing us in

a specific direction. Just take a closer look at this photo of Fenn with his horse that he provided in his book "TTOTC". The "blaze" on his horse even looks like an arrow pointing down. Remember, *"If you've been wise and found the blaze, look quickly down your quest to cease"*.

I personally like this option and will keep it in mind when searching for the "blaze".

Photo Credit: Rock on the Madison River. Jim Belote ©2009

A scar (carving or painting) on a rock?

You know how I feel about this one. A "blaze" on a large rock fits the bill to a "t" (or maybe a cross "†"). You have something that is extremely plausible because it's face could be carved or painted on, it is considered a natural rock formation and not a man-made object (although the actual carving or painting on it could be), it can be seen during the day without a flashlight, it has longevity as it most likely will be around for hundreds to thousands of years, and it also can be removed, but is not very feasible to do so. A large rock could also host a number of either carved or painted objects such as; an "X" or cross "†", the blaze on a horse (see above photo), and even double Omegas. And Fenn might have even hinted about the "blaze" being a carving, because on page 177 in one of his books, there is a photo of a hammer and Stone Carver's chisel. Hmm. Could that be a hint?

Photo credit: "The Thrill of the Chase" by Forrest Fenn

An "X" or a "†" (cross)?

The above photo is actually the drawing of a graveyard that appears on the bottom of page 41 in Fenn's book "TTOTC". If you look closely, you see a cross (circled in red) that is sticking out of the ground and is slightly rotated also giving it the appearance of being an "X".

Well, let's look at the facts:

1. The letter "X" is the only letter of the alphabet NOT used in Fenn's poem.

2. The letter "X" is the Roman numeral for the number 10. Fenn's poem contains 9 clues so maybe the "X" could represent the 10th and final clue which marks the spot of the treasure chest.

3. An "X" or a cross "†" can be carved or painted on a tree or rock face.

136

4. It can be radial. An "X" turned on its side can form a cross and vise-versa. But, since a cross "†" usually has one line longer than the other, that longer line can be used to radially point straight down or to any other direction desired.

5. It can be one object that satisfies two meanings.

a. "X" MARKS THE SPOT.
An "X" usually marks the spot of a treasure on a treasure map and Fenn has previously said his poem was a map. Is this the end of our quest for his treasure?
IF YOU HAVE BEEN WISE (SMART) AND FOUND THE BLAZE (an "X" = THE TREASURE MARKER)

and

b. A CROSS "†" IS A GRAVE MARKER.
A cross "†" is a symbol that can be used to mark the spot of someone who is deceased. Could this mark the end of Fenn's rainbow? Could a cross "†" be carved or painted on a large stone to symbolize a grave stone or grave marker located at Fenn's "secret" treasure hiding spot which is near his "secret" fishing hole?
IF YOU HAVE BEEN WISE (SPIRITUAL) AND FOUND THE BLAZE (A CROSS "†" = FENN'S GRAVE MARKER)

All I can say about this possibility is…WOW!

Double Omegas?

What is an Omega? If you are a spiritual or a religious person, you definitely would have heard the term "Alpha and Omega", which is used by Christians as a title for Jesus and symbolizes "Alpha" as the beginning and "Omega" as the end.

Why would double Omegas be used as the "blaze"? The reason double Omegas are a possible option as the "blaze" is because those symbols appear in the back of Fenn's book "TTOTC" and many searchers believe they have a hidden or special meaning to Fenn. I see where they are going with that, because in a way they might. The double Omegas would not only symbolize two endings to Fenn's book and poem, but also continue Fenn's use of the double entendre.

1. THE END OF MY RAINBOW.
The end of Fenn's fishing rod. The end of his story. The end of his journey through life.
and
2. THE TREASURE.
The end of the directions in the poem. The end of your quest for the treasure chest.

A Totem Pole?

A Totem Pole? How would anyone get the idea it could be a totem pole? First, it would be wise to discuss what a totem and a totem pole actually is.

Totem:
1. An object (such as an animal or plant) serving as the emblem of a family or clan (especially Native Americans) and often as a reminder of its ancestry; also: A usually carved or painted representation of such an object.
2. One that serves as an emblem or revered symbol.

Totem Pole:
1. Monumental sculptures carved on poles, posts, or pillars with symbols or figures made from large trees. Given the complexity and symbolic meanings of totem pole carvings, their placement and importance lie in the observer's knowledge and connection to the meanings of the figures and the culture in which they are embedded. The rarest type of totem pole is a mortuary pole. It incorporates grave boxes with carved supporting poles or includes a recessed back to hold the grave box. It is among the tallest, reaching 50 to 70 feet in height.

I know that this is just drawing at straws, but here are a few of the reasons why I believe some searchers have associated Fenn's "blaze" with a totem pole.

1. In Fenn' book "TTOTC", there is a chapter titled "The Totem Café Caper"
2. Fenn worked at the Totem Café in West Yellowstone, MT.
3. Even thou Fenn was the middle child according to their ages, Fenn was considered the "low man on the totem pole" within his family hierarchy according to his father. Fenn could actually sit and die under a real Totem Pole with his treasure chest.
4. Fenn has a passion for Native American lands and artifacts.

An Arrowhead?

Why an arrowhead? Fenn's first ever treasure was an arrowhead which he found at the age of nine. He has a passion for Native American artifacts and supposedly he still has that arrowhead and considers it to be one of his prized possessions.

Also, an arrowhead can be radial, and if mounted to a tree or rock could be placed specifically to point down or in any direction Fenn would want it to.

The problem is that it would be a little difficult to see and also have no longevity as it is not only fragile, but could be easily removed and taken.

In the end, to me, it just doesn't make sense that the "blaze" would be an arrowhead.

An intensely burning fire?

Well, unless Fenn has discovered the eternal flame, I think a lack of longevity is only one of the reasons that make it easy to rule out the possibility of the "blaze" being an intensely burning fire. Not to mention its plausibility…it would be dangerous. But I'm sure there would be at least one searcher out there finding a "blaze" and looking down into it thinking the treasure chest is actually in the fire. If you're that person, I guess my words of wisdom for you would be,

"STOP, DROP, AND ROLL."

An intensely burning fire as the "blaze" is a big fat "NO" from me.

What do I think Fenn's "blaze" can be?

Q: Mr. Fenn, Which direction does the Blaze face? North, South, East or West? Curious.

"I didn't take a radial off of the blaze Foxy. I'm thinking it may not be any of those directions." FF

According to its use in surveying, a radial line a line passing through the center of a circle, cylinder, or sphere. The correct "direction" of the radial line is from the radius point to a point on the arc of a circle. A couple examples of this would be a radial tire or even the arms on a clock face (which could point in many radial directions).

IS THE "BLAZE" DIRECTIONAL? Could the "blaze" be on a tree or a rock face pointing down or in the direction of the treasure chest? Absolutely.

My "blaze" had to satisfy the following assumptions:

1. It has to be on a natural object that has longevity and can stand the test of time. (A LARGE ROCK OR BOULDER)
2. It has to satisfy two meanings. (A SCAR, CARVING, OR PAINTING ON A ROCK THAT LOOKS LIKE SOMETHING RECOGNIZABLE LIKE THE BLAZE OF A HORSE, AN "X" OR A CROSS "†", OR EVEN DOUBLE OMEGAS)
3. It has to possibly be something that can be considered to be radial (or directional) to point me in the right direction. (AN "X" OR A CROSS "†" OR THE BLAZE ON A HORSE)

Also, since Fenn said "if <u>you have</u> been wise and <u>found</u> the blaze", I believe you can see Fenn's "blaze" before the four descriptive lines in his poem barring you have great vision (like an owl), or at the very least, binoculars.

My "blaze"

As I confidently approached my search area along the Madison River (about 10 miles downstream from Madison Junction), I quickly noticed something of interest.

DO YOU SEE IT? IS THAT THE "BLAZE"?

No...not the rock protruding out of the waters of the Madison River.

The Rock directly across the Madison River.

Since my solution has me crossing the Madison River at the right spot and I did not have binoculars, I used my phone's camera in an attempt to get a closer look at exactly what I was seeing across the river.

Is it a mirage?

Is my phone camera deceiving me?

Are my own two eyes deceiving me?

Do I see a rock "blaze"?

More specifically, do I see a rock "blaze" with the "blaze of a horse"? That surely would satisfy two meanings of the word "blaze" and still considered a single object, right?
1. A scar on a rock.
and
2. That scar happens to look like the "blaze" of a horse.

Could Fenn's treasure chest be sitting right there, directly down, under that scar, sitting on a ledge "in" but not "under" the cooling waters of the Madison River?

I WAS ABOUT TO FIND OUT...

NOPE.

Unfortunately, while it was a scar on a rock, it did not resemble what I thought to be a blaze of a horse nor was there a treasure chest to be found within its vicinity.

Where did I go wrong? The funny thing about that is that I can actually think of two reasons I didn't find it.
1. I OVERCOOKED THE POEM.
or
2. I HAVE THE WRONG "WHERE WARM WATERS HALT".

Too bad I don't know how to play Canasta.

Even though I didn't find the treasure chest, let's finish up with my analysis and interpretation of Fenn's poem as it may offer an extra hint or two.

Look quickly down, your quest to cease,

INSTRUCTIONS

LOOK

QUICKLY

DOWN
1. Downstream.
2. Below or in a lower position or elevation.
3. Southerly direction (South).

YOUR

QUEST
1. A long or arduous search for something. (journey, search, hunt, pursuit)

TO
1. Into a position that is closed or almost closed.

CEASE
1. To cause to come to an end especially gradually.
2. Bring or come to an end. (halt. stop)

LOOK QUICKLY DOWN
1. YOUR QUEST IS COMING TO AN END.
and
2. FORREST FENN'S JOURNEY THROUGH LIFE IS COMING TO AN END. (IF APPLICABLE)

But tarry scant with marvel gaze,

INSTRUCTIONS

BUT

TARRY
1. To linger, remain or stay in or at a place.
2. Of, like, or covered with tar.

SCANT
1. Very little, very few. Barely sufficient or adequate. (adjective)
2. (Masonry) A block of stone sawn on two sides to bed level.
Noun
3. (Masonry) A sheet of stone.
4. (Wood) A slightly thinner measurement of a standard wood style.

WITH

MARVEL

GAZE
1. To fix the eyes in a steady intent look often with eagerness or studious attention. (Stare)

1. BUT, DON'T STAY AROUND THERE VERY LONG AND STARE AT THE TREASURE CHEST.
and
2. BUT, DON'T STAY AROUND THERE VERY LONG AND STARE AT FORREST FENN'S BONES.
(IF APPLICABLE)

147

Just take the chest and go in peace.

INSTRUCTIONS

JUST (Only)

TAKE THE CHEST AND GO IN

PEACE
1. Used interjectionally to ask for silence.
2. Used interjectionally as a greeting or farewell.

1. JUST TAKE THE TREASURE CHEST AND GO QUIETLY. SHH! (GREETINGS TREASURE)
and
2. JUST LEAVE FORREST FENN'S BONES AND GO IN PEACE. AMEN. (FAREWELL FORREST FENN)
(IF APPLICABLE)

148

"And into the forest I go, to lose my mind and find my soul."
John Muir

So why is it that I must go
And leave my trove for all to seek?

QUESTION

SO

WHY
1. For what reason or purpose.

IS

IT

THAT

I (Forrest Fenn)

MUST

GO
1. Leave, Depart. To physically go away. (Alive)
2. Depart. Die. To spiritually go away. (Death)

AND

LEAVE
1. Allow to remain. Abandon. Desert. (Standard definition)
2. Bequeath. Leave (a personal estate or one's body) to a person or other beneficiary by a will. Pass (something) on or leave (something) to someone else. (Legal definition)

MY (Forrest Fenn)

TROVE
*1. A store of valuable or delightful things. A collection of objects.
(Standard definition)
2. Treasure-trove: Any money, bullion, or the like, of unknown
ownership, found hidden in the earth or any other place: In the
absence of statutory provisions to the contrary it may be kept by
the finder. (Legal definition)*

FOR

ALL
1. Everybody.

TO

SEEK
1. Attempt to find (something).

**1. SO WHY IS IT THAT I (FORREST FENN) MUST GO
(PHYSICALLY LEAVE) AND LEAVE MY TROVE
(ALLOW MY TREASURE CHEST TO REMAIN) FOR
ALL TO SEEK?**
and
**2. SO WHY IS IT THAT I (FORREST FENN) MUST GO
(SPIRITUALLY DEPART, DIE) AND LEAVE
(BEQUEATH) MY TROVE (TREASURE CHEST) FOR
ALL TO SEEK?
(IF APPLICABLE)**

The answers I already know, I've done it tired, and now I'm weak.

ANSWERS

THE

ANSWERS (Plural, multiple answers)

I (Forrest Fenn)

ALREADY

KNOW

1. I'VE DONE IT TIRED (past tense)

AND

2. NOW I'M WEAK (present tense)

THE ANSWERS I (FORREST FENN) ALREADY KNOW,
1. I'VE HID THE TREASURE CHEST TIRED.
and
2. NOW I'M TOO WEAK TO RETURN.

So hear me all and listen good,

INSTRUCTIONS

SO

HEAR

ME

ALL
1. Everybody.

AND

LISTEN

GOOD
1. Close.

SO
1. HEAR ME EVERYBODY.
and
2. LISTEN CLOSELY.

Your effort will be worth the cold.

POSSIBLE HINT (FUTURE TENSE)

YOUR

EFFORT
1. Strenuous mental exertion.
2. Strenuous physical exertion.

WILL BE (Future tense)

WORTH

THE

COLD
1. Of or at a low or relatively low temperature, especially when compared with the human body (e.g. cold air temperature, cold body temperature, cold water temperature.
2. lacking affection or warmth of feeling; unemotional.

> *"Stay out of the mountains in the winter time when it is cold and snow covers the ground." FF*

Here Fenn says stay out of the mountains when it is "cold". I thought my "effort" was supposed to be "worth the cold" according to his poem. I believe he is referring to the "cold" waters of a river, stream, or creek.

YOUR <u>MENTAL</u> AND <u>PHYSICAL</u> EXERTION WILL BE (FUTURSE TENSE) WORTH THE COLD (<u>BODY</u> AND <u>WATER</u> TEMPERATURE).

If you are brave and in the wood

POSSIBLE HINT (PRESENT TENSE)

IF

YOU

ARE (Present tense)

BRAVE
1. Ready to face (unpleasant conditions) and endure danger or pain; showing courage.
2. Having or showing mental or moral strength to face danger, fear, or difficulty.

AND

IN

THE

WOOD
1. An area of land, smaller than a forest, that is covered with growing trees.
2. The hard-fibrous material that is the main substance of the trunk/branches of a tree. (Hidden in a hollow log?)
3. The inside of the treasure chest? The chest has a wood lining.
In my opinion, you have to be physically inside the treasure chest to receive legal ownership to the gold.

IF YOU ARE CURRENTLY <u>MENTALLY</u> AND <u>PHYSICALLY</u> STRONG AND IN THE WOOD (INSIDE THE CHEST)

I give you title to the gold.

LEGAL AFFIRMATION

I (Forrest Fenn)

GIVE

YOU

TITLE
1. A legal just cause of exclusive possession.
2. All the elements constituting legal ownership.
3. A form of ownership free of valid claims by other parties.
4. The aggregate evidence that gives rise to a legal right of possession or control.

TO

THE

GOLD

I (FORREST FENN) GIVE YOU TITLE (LEGAL OWNERSHIP) TO THE GOLD.

Contract:
1. A written or spoken agreement, especially one concerning employment, sales, tenancy, or any other property (something owned or possessed), that is to be enforceable by law.

No matter whether Fenn is still alive or deceased when his treasure chest is found, he is using the poem as a written contract, giving the finder legal ownership to the gold.

157

Fenn has said he would know if the treasure chest has been found. But how?

Who knows for sure, but I think he has informants.

No matter where you go in Yellowstone National Park, there are eyes watching your every move.

Chapter 4:
MY TWO CENTS...LITERALLY

Upon arriving at my hotel room in West Yellowstone, Montana, I immediately found a shiny penny on the floor. You know what they say about that? "Find a penny and pick it up and all day you will have good luck." That put a big smile on my face and made the beginning of my adventure that much better.

Thinking I had just added luck to my side since I already had the bravery and confidence to make the trip, it was time to head out. Now, Fenn said that you are supposed to go only where a 79 or an 80-year-old man can go. So, instead of just trying to envision the physical capabilities of a gentleman that age, I decided to bring one with me...my father. I knew that if we were in an area that he could not make it through, my solution wouldn't be invalid. But that was not the case as we had zero difficulty following the map I created from Fenn's poem.

It was a beautiful sunny day as we drove to my search area located along the Madison River in Yellowstone National Park. As soon as we arrived, it just felt right. Peaceful, secluded, and tranquil, as the only sound you could hear is the sound of the river. And how could you not fall in love with the view...

And while I didn't take as many photos as I would have liked to, I could not resist taking the ones I did. I mean, one of the main reasons I went on this trip in the first place was to get away from my computer and phone for a few days and just be present in the moment and not get distracted and disconnected by viewing the beautiful scenery through digital eyes.

As we made our way along the south bank of the Madison River, I couldn't help but notice something suspicious.

Is that the "blaze"?

Did Fenn just get lazy at the end of his journey and just nail a piece of wood to a tree pointing down?

NOPE.

And yes, I still did take a look around there for Fenn's treasure chest anyway.

We continued on our way talking loudly, so the animals knew we were there, and discussing what we would do when we found the treasure and also what we would hope for if someone else had already found it before me.

Here are the things I would love to see when the treasure is found.

1. Me or another finder returns Fenn's turquoise bracelet to him or to his family (possibly his grandson Shiloh) if he has passed.

2. The treasure chest stays mostly intact (with the exception of the returned bracelet and his auto-biography that is inside of an olive jar sealed with wax) and is sold to a museum so it can be viewed and enjoyed by everyone.

3. Fenn's auto-biography, that is inside of an olive jar sealed with wax, gets published with a percentage of the profits going to cancer research.

I think that would make me or another finder happy, the many other searchers out there happy, and hopefully would make Mr. Forrest Fenn and his family happy.

And just like that, we quickly reached our destination. As I made my way to the water's edge, I realized I could have just left my father in the car, because you already know what I saw and what I found.

Nothing...or did I?

Although I didn't find Forrest Fenn's treasure, I didn't walk away empty handed either. As I sat down at the gate in the airport awaiting my flight home, I took a few minutes to reflect on the amazing experience I just had. That is when I looked down and I noticed it...another penny. Like I said before "Find a penny and pick it up and all day you will have good luck." That put a big smile on my face and just made the end of my adventure that much better.

Did I find the treasure?
NO.

Did Fenn make me hate the English language?

Did I find a greater appreciation for the solitude and tranquility of nature?

Do I still think the chest is hidden out there?

Do I think I was searching the right area?

Do I think I was close?

Did Fenn lure me like one of his Brown trout?

Will I go out searching again?

Well...YES.
But that's just my two cents.

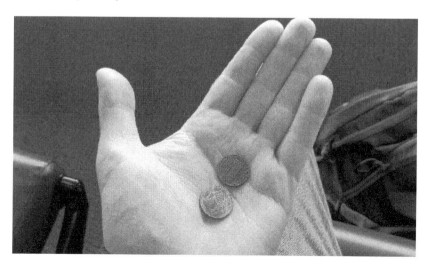

"I hope parents will take their children camping and hiking in the Rocky Mountains. I hope they will fish, look for fossils, turn rotten logs over to see what's under them, and look for my treasure." Forrest Fenn

Made in the USA
Columbia, SC
17 November 2019